In the name of Allah, Most Gracious, Most Merciful

One Hundred Incredible Virtues of Ali bin Abi Taleb and His Sons

Ibn Shazan

Translated by Sayyid Mohsen Milani

www.shiabooks.ca

Author's Dedication:

To whom should I dedicate this?

This is a humble whisper to none other than my master and my commander, the one who received a present from the Magnificent Lord, who said "This is a present from the Victorious Lord to Ali bin Abi Taleb."[1]

---

[1] This is referring to a HADITH that Al-Hafez Al-Dailami narrated in his book, FERDOUS (a manuscript), that Abdul Razzaq narrated from Mo'ammar, from Al-Zohari, from Arafah bin Al-Zubair, from Ibn Abbas, who said:

When Ali bin Abi Taleb killed Amro Bin Abdewad Al-Amery, he came to the Prophet with his sword still dripping with the blood of Amr.

When the Messenger of God saw Ali he said, "O Allah, give Ali some qualities that you have not given to anyone else before him and that you will not give to anyone after him."

So Jibraeel came down with a tangerine from Paradise. He told the Prophet, "The Magnificent Lord sends His salaam to you and says, 'Give greetings to Ali bin Abi Taleb with this tangerine from Me."

The Prophet gave the tangerine to Ali bin Abi Taleb and it split into two halves. There was a green silk cloth in the tangerine that had the following written on it, "This is a present from the Victorious Lord to Ali bin Abi Taleb."

(Kharazmi in Manaqeb P105. Dhahabi in Mizan Al-Eetedal V1 P76. Qondoozi in Yanabee Al-Mawaddah P95.)

About the Author, Ibn Shazan

Ibn Shazan was one of the great scholars of the fifth century who safe-guarded the inheritance and knowledge of the Ahlul Bayt for us by writing and publishing several works that share this treasure.

This book specifically has had a great impact in the Muslim world because the author has carefully selected the sources from Sunni books, thereby eliminating any question of impartiality.

Those who study the history of Islam find that occasionally, paid writers try to create doubt in the peoples' hearts with their poisonous books. It is our scholars who fight them with precious and authentic publications, such as this one, which is void of any personal opinion.

There are two editions of this book. The first is in the library of Ayatullah Sayyid Mustafa Al-Khounsari and the second one is in the library of Ayatullah Al-Maraashi Al-Najafi.

The following are some of Ibn Shazan's other valuable publications:

1. Eidhaah Dafaen Al-Nawaseb
2. Al-Ekhtelaf fi Wahdat Al-Kattabeen
3. Raddul Shams Aala Amir Al-Moemenin
4. Al-Manaqeb

Note from the Author, Ibn Shazan

In the name of Allah, Most Gracious, Most Merciful

Praise be to the Lord, who was the first without beginning and is the last without an end, the Just in His judgment, the Merciful Lord, the Only Owner that does not need anyone; He is close to His slaves while being extremely High. This is the praise of someone who knows praising is mandatory and forgetting it is a sin; this is the belief of someone who knows that his deeds depend on his beliefs, someone who could not exist without hope in his Lord's mercy.

I rely on the Lord as someone who believes that there is no will nor power except from God. I testify that there is no god but Allah, and I testify this until I die, and I hope that this saves me at difficult times. And I testify that Mohammadﷺ is His slave and Messenger; he is the Prophet of Mercy, he is the light of the nation and he is the nations' saviour from ignorance and blindness. Salawat of Allah be on him and on his family with no limit and with no measure.

I have collected these incredible virtues of the Commander of the Believers, the Leader of the believers, and the Lion of the Glorious Lord, Ali bin Abi Taleb؏. I have collected them from Sunni books. Hold on to them firmly and learn them thoroughly. They are short so the reader cannot complain of boredom. May Allah help us find the right path and may He not keep us away from Paradise.

Note from Translator, Sayyid Mohsen Milani

In the name of Allah, Most Gracious, Most Merciful

This book is an extremely valuable Shia resource. Every effort has been made to ensure that nothing has been lost in its translation from Arabic to English.

It is very important to understand that these are AHADITH of the Prophetﷺ, and as God says in the Holy Qur'an, "Nor does he [The Prophet] speak out of his (own) desire. It is but a revelation revealed." (53:3-4)

The following suggestions may provide a richer reading of this book:

1. Look at the source of the HADITH (the last person in the top portion of each virtue). This will allow you to get a better understanding of the tone that the Prophetﷺ adopts in each HADITH.

2. Pay attention to the difference in quality, tone, etc. of the AHADITH that are from God directly compared to others.

3. Try to read each virtue more than once until you fully absorb the meaning of the HADITH. The reader's goal should not be to finish this book; it should be to learn it.

The sources of each virtue are mentioned at the bottom of the page and all of these sources are in Arabic. If one of the sources has been translated the page numbers may not match the Arabic version exactly.

I kindly ask all of those who read this book to recite Surah Al-Fateha for the author of this book, the great scholar, **Ibn Shazan.**

The reader can find this and other valuable Shia books at:

www.shiabooks.ca

Virtue #1

Hasan bin Ahmad, son of Sokhtoeh, narrated in Kufa, in the year of three hundred and seventy four, from Abu Bakr Mohammad bin Ahmad bin Isa bin Mihran, from Yahya bin Abdul Hamid, from Qays bin Rabee, from Aamash, from Abaya, from Habba Al-A'arni, from the Commander of the Believers, Ali bin Abi Taleb ﷺ, who said:

The Messenger of God ﷺ said:

I am the master of the first and the last, and you, O Ali, are the master of the creation after me. I am just like you and you are just like me.[1]

Virtue #2

Abu Zakariyya Talha bin Ahmad bin Talha bin Mohammad Al-Sarram narrated that a hajji came to Kufa and narrated from Abu Ma'aad Shah bin Abdul Rahman, from Ali bin Abdullah, from Abdul Hamid Al-Qatad, from Hashim bin Bashir, from Shaba bin Al-Hajjaj, from Oday bin Thabet, from Saeed bin Jubair, from Ibn Abbas, who said: .

The Messenger of God ﷺ said:

Ali bin Abi Taleb is God's best creation after me. Hasan and Husain are the Masters of the Youth of Paradise, and their father enjoys an even higher status than they do, and Fatema is the Master of all of the Worlds' Women.[2]

Virtue #3

Abul Tayyeb Mohammad bin Husain narrated from Mohammad bin Suleiman, from Yahya bin Ahmad, from Mohammad bin Mutawakkil, from

---

[1] Bihar V25 P360 H17. Ghayatol Maram P450 H14 and P620 H17. Khawarazmi in Manaqeb P31 and in Maqtal V1 P39. Yanabee Al-Mawaddah 133. Kashf Al-Ghammah V1 P103. Ehqaq al-Haq V6 P111. Misbah Al-Anwar P61.
[2] Sadouq in Khesal P206 H25. Bihar V43 P26 H24. Ibn Shahr Ahoub in Manaqeb V3 P103. Sadough in Maani AL-Akhbar P107 H1. Qonduzi in Yanabee Al-Mawaddah P260. Awalem V11 P44. Dailami in Ferdous. Soyoutti in Tarikh Al-Kholafa P 114. Ibn Abi Al-Hadid in Sharh Nahj Al-Balagha V2 P457. Helyatol Awliya V2 P42. Khawarazmi in Maqtal V1 P79. Mashkal Al-Athar V1 P48. Moheb Al-Deen Al-Tabari in Dhakhaer Al-Oqba P 43. Mo'tasar min Al-Mokhtasar V2 P147. Dhahabi in Tarikh Al-Islam V2 P 91. Wasilatol Amal P80. Rashfat Al-Sadi 226. Estiaab V4 P385. Esabah V4 P378. Sirat Al-Nabaviyat V2 P6. Mashareq Al-Anwar P105. Osod Al-Ghaba V5 P522.

Zufr bin Al-Hathil, from Aamash, from Mowarreq, from Jabir bin Abdullah Al-Ansari, who said:

The Messenger of God﷽ said:

Hasan﷽ was named Al-Hasan (beneficent) because God kept the skies from falling on earth with His Beneficence.[3] Ali and Hasan are both names which are derived from Allah's names, and Husain is a derivative of Hasan.[4]

Virtue #4

Ahmad bin Mohammad bin Jarrah narrated from the judge, Amr bin Al-Husain, from Aminah Bint Ahmad bin Dhahl bin Suleiman Al-Aamash, from her father, from Suleiman bin Mehran, from Mohammad bin Katheer, from Abu Khaithame, from Abdullah son of Omar, who said:

The Messenger of God﷽ said:

I am your Warner and Ali bin Abi Taleb﷽ is your guide. "Verily you are a Warner and for every group there is a guide" (13:7). Through Hasan, you receive God's beneficence and through Husain﷽ you will achieve either salvation or damnation. Husain﷽ is a door from the doors of Paradise; God has made the smell of Paradise HARAAM (unlawful) on those who fight Husain.[5]

Virtue #5

Mohammad bin Ali bin Fadl bin Tamam Al-Zaiat narrated from Mohammad bin Qassem, from Abbad bin Yacoub, from Musa bin Uthman, from Aamash, from Abu Ishaq, from Hareth and Saeed, sons of Qays, from Ali bin Abi Taleb﷽, who said:

The Messenger of God﷽ said:

I will be at the Pool of Kawthar on the Day of Judgement and you, O Ali, will

---

[3] Note from Translator: The Imams represent God's virtues and one of God's virtues is "Beneficence." Imam Hasan ﷽ represents God's Beneficence. Imam Hasan ﷽ is the reason that the skies do not fall to the earth. Refer to Ziarat Al-Jamea Al-Kabeera.
[4] Madinatol Ma'ajez P202 H4 and P238 H8. Helyatol Abrar V1 P499. Bihar V43 P252. A'walem P16. Manaqeb Ibn Shahr Ashoub V3 P166
[5] Bihar V35 P405 H28. Ghayatol Maram P235 H6. Borhan V2 P181. Kharazmi in Maqtal V1 P14

distribute the water. Hasan⁽ᵃˢ⁾ will keep people away from the Pool; Husain⁽ᵃˢ⁾ will give the orders; Ali bin Husain⁽ᵃˢ⁾ will be the enforcer; Mohammad bin Ali⁽ᵃˢ⁾ will be the revealer; Jaafar bin Mohammad⁽ᵃˢ⁾ will be the driver; Musa bin Jaafar⁽ᵃˢ⁾ will be counting the lovers and the resentful, and he will be the destroyer of the hypocrites; Ali bin Musa⁽ᵃˢ⁾ will beautify the believers; Mohammad bin Ali⁽ᵃˢ⁾ will award degrees to the inhabitants of Paradise; Ali bin Mohammad⁽ᵃˢ⁾ will be the preacher of his Shia and he will marry them from HUR AL-EEN, "Pure maidens with big beautiful eyes" (56:22); Hasan bin Ali⁽ᵃˢ⁾ will be the light of the inhabitants of Paradise - they will see with his light; and the Qaem⁽ᵃˢ⁾ (12th Imam) will be the intercessor who will ask God to allow them (the believers) to enter Paradise on the Day of Judgement, a day on which God will accept only the intercession of those with whom He is pleased.[6][7]

Virtue #6

Mohammad bin Abdullah bin Ubaidullah bin Morrah narrated from Abdullah bin Mohammad Al-Baghawey, from Ali bin Al-Jaad, from Ahmad bin Wahab bin Mansour, from Abu Qobisa Shuraih bin Mohammad Al-Anbari from Nafi', from Abdullah bin Omar Ibn Al-Khattab, who said:

The Messenger of God⁽ˢ⁾ said to Ali bin Abi Taleb⁽ᵃˢ⁾:

O Ali! I am the Warner of my nation; you are their guide; Hasan⁽ᵃˢ⁾ is the leader (of my nation); Husain⁽ᵃˢ⁾ is the driver; Ali bin Husain⁽ᵃˢ⁾ unites the nation; Mohammad bin Ali⁽ᵃˢ⁾ is the most informed of my nation; Jaafar bin Mohammad⁽ᵃˢ⁾ is its writer; Musa bin Jaafar⁽ᵃˢ⁾ is its counter; Ali bin Musa⁽ᵃˢ⁾ is the nations' cross guard and its saviour, and he banishes those who are resentful of the nation, and he draws the believers from my nation close together; Mohammad bin Ali⁽ᵃˢ⁾ drives my nation; Ali bin Mohammad⁽ᵃˢ⁾ is the most knowledgeable of my nation and its protector; Hasan bin Ali⁽ᵃˢ⁾ is the caller of my nation and is the most generous of my nation; and the Qaem⁽ᵃˢ⁾ (12th Imam) is the cupbearer and the beseeched.

---

⁶ Note from Translator: Each one of these titles represents a virtue from God's virtues. These titles are not necessarily linked to the Pool of Kawthar or the Day of Judgement. Some describe a few of the roles that an Imam performs in this life, on the Day of Judgement, and/or in Paradise. These roles are not the only roles that Imams have on the Day of Judgement, and/or in Paradise. Some of these titles are given to the Imams because of the way they were treated in this world.
⁷ Kharazmi in Maqtal V1 P94. Taraef P173. Sirat Al-Mostaqim V2 P150. Helyatol Abrar V2 P721. Ghayatol Maram P35 H22 and P692 H2. Faraed Al-Semtayn V2 P231 H572. Bihar V36 P270

Then he (the Prophet﴿ﷺ﴾) said, "O Abdullah (son of Omar), 'Verily in this are signs for those who examine it closely" (15:75).[8][9]

Virtue #7

Sahl bin Ahmad narrated from Abu Jaafar Mohammad bin Jarir Al-Taabari, from Hinad bin Al-Serri, from Mohammad bin Hisham, from Saeed son of Abi Saeed, from Mohammad bin Monkader, from Jabir bin Abdullah Al-Ansari, who said:

The Messenger of God ﷺ said:

When God created the heavens and the earth He called on them and they responded. He presented my Prophethood and the WILAYAT of Ali bin Abi Taleb to them, both of which they accepted. Then God created the creatures and entrusted the religious affairs to us. Therefore, the happy ones are those who are happy with us, and the unhappy are those who are unhappy with us. We permit that which God has made HALAL (lawful) and prohibit that which God has deemed HARAAM.[10]

Virtue #8

The judge, Al-Moaafi bin Zakariyya, narrated from Abdullah bin Mohammad bin Abdullah bin Al-Aziz Al-Baghawey, from Yahya Al-Hamani, from Mohammad bin Al Fadeel, from Al-Kalbi, from Abi Saleh, from Ibn Abbas, who said:

One day I was sitting in front of the Prophet ﷺ, Ali ﵇, Fatema ﵇, Hasan and Husain ﵇ when Angel Jibraeel came down and greeted the Prophet ﷺ with an apple.

The Prophet ﷺ accepted the greeting by taking the apple. The Prophet ﷺ then greeted Ali ﵇ and gave him the apple. Ali bin Abi Taleb ﵇ accepted the greeting by taking the apple. He kissed the apple and then returned it to the Messenger of God ﷺ. The Prophet ﷺ accepted his greeting by taking the apple.

---

[8] Note from Translator: Refer to note number 2 from translator.
[9] Bihar V36 P280. Manaqeb Shar Ahoub V1 P251. Ethbatol Hodat V3 P222 through 34 different ways. Sirat Al-Mostaqim V2 P150
[10] Ghayatol Maram P208 H9. Kharazmi in Manaqeb P79 and in Maqtal V1 P46.Al-Mohtazer P97. Kashf Al-Ghomma V1 P291. Misbah Al-Anwar P64.Bihar V17 P13 H25.

Then the Prophet greeted Hasan and gave him the apple. Hasan accepted the greeting by taking the apple. He kissed the apple and then returned it to the Messenger of God. The Prophet accepted his greeting.

Then the Prophet greeted Husain and gave him the apple. Husain accepted the greeting by taking the apple. He kissed the apple and then returned it to the Messenger of God. The Prophet accepted his greeting.

Then the Prophet greeted Fatema and gave her the apple. Fatema accepted the greeting by taking the apple. She kissed the apple and then returned it to the Messenger of God. The Prophet accepted her greeting.

The Prophet greeted Ali again and gave him the apple. Ali accepted his greeting and kissed the apple. In an effort to return the apple to the Prophet, the apple fell from his fingertips. The apple split into two halves and from it, a light shone until it reached the sky.

The following message was written inside the apple:

> In the name of Allah, Most Gracious, Most Merciful. This is a greeting from Allah to the chosen Mohammad and to Ali Al-Murtadha, and Fatema Al-Zahra'a, and Hasan and Husain, the grandsons of the Prophet. This letter is a guarantee to their lovers of protection from the fire on the Day of Judgement.[11]

Virtue #9

Nuh bin Ahmad bin Ayman narrated from Ibrahim bin Ahmad bin Abi Hasin, from his grandfather, from Yahya bin Abdul Hamid, from Qays bin Rabee, from Suleiman Al-Aamash, from Jaafar bin Mohammad (Imam Al-Sadiq), from my father, from Ali bin Husain, from his father, from my father, the Commander of the Believers, who said:

The Messenger of God told me:

O Ali, you are the Commander of the Believers and the Imam of the pious. O Ali, you are the master of all of the successors of the prophets.

---

[11] Ghayatol Maram P659. Madinatol Ma'jiz P61 H131. Kharazmin in Maqtal V1 P95. Bihar V43 P308 H72. A'walim V16 P62. Sadouq in his Amal P477. Jawahir Al-Saniyya P233.

You inherit all of the prophets' knowledge and you are the best of SEDDIQIN (the truthful ones) and the best of those who believed in God first.

O Ali, you are the husband of the woman who is the Master of all of the Worlds' Women, and you are the successor of the best of the prophets.

O Ali, you are the Master of the Believers.

O Ali, you are the evidence that proves God's existence after me on all people. Those who follow you will earn Paradise, and those who are against you deserve Hell.

O Ali, I swear to God, who sent me as a Prophet and who chose me from among all of His creatures, if any slave worships God for a thousand years, God will not accept it unless he believes in your WILAYAT and the WILAYAT of your sons[12]. Furthermore, your WILAYAT will not be accepted unless it is accompanied with the hate of your enemies and the enemies of your sons[13]. This is what Angel Jibraeel has told me.

Let them choose to be believers or KAFERS (disbelievers).[14]

Virtue #10

Sahl bin Ahmad narrated from Ali bin Abdullah, from Al-Zubairi Ishaq bin Ibrahim, from Abdul Razzaq bin Hamam, from his father, from Mina, slave of Abdul Rahman bin Awf, from Abdullah bin Masoud, who said:

I was with the Messenger of God 🕌, when he sighed heavily.

"O the Messenger of God, why are you so sad?" I asked.

"O Ibn Masoud, my death is approaching," the Prophet 🕌 replied.

"Appoint a successor, O Messenger of God," I said.

"Who?" The Prophet 🕌 asked.

"Abu Bakr," I replied.

---

[12] Note from Translator: God does not accept anyone's deeds who does not believe in the WILAYAT.
[13] Note from Translator: God does not accept the belief in the WILAYAT without the HATE of the enemies of the AHLUL-BAYT.
[14] Al-Yaqeen P56. Bihar V27 P199 H66. Ghayatol Maram P17 H9. Ithbatol Hodat V4 P168 H507. Kanz Al-Ommal P185. Mostadrak V1 P23. Rowzat Al-Jannat V6 P183.

The Prophet🕮 fell silent and sighed heavily again.

"Why you are so sad? O the Messenger of God, I will sacrifice myself for you," I said.

"My death is approaching," replied the Prophet🕮.

"Appoint a successor," I said.

"Who will it be?" asked the Prophet🕮.

"Omar bin Al-Khattab," I replied.

The Prophet🕮 fell silent and sighed heavily for the third time.

"I will ransom my mother and father for you. Why are you so sad, O the Messenger of God?" I asked.

"My death is approaching", replied the Prophet🕮.

"Appoint a successor," I said.

"Who will it be?" asked the Prophet🕮.

"Ali bin Abi Taleb," I said.

Then the Prophet🕮 cried and said, "Ah, you people will not obey him! If you would, God would allow you into Paradise. But by disobeying him, God will remove the value from anything good that you do."[15]

Virtue #11

Qutaibah bin Saeed Abu Raja narrated from Nafi', from Abdullah bin Omar bin Al-Khattab, who said:

The Messenger of God🕮 said to Ali🕮:

---

[15] Ghayatol Maram P69 H14. Kharazmi in Manaqeb P64. Faraed Al-Semtain V1 P167 H209. Tousi in Amal V1 P313. Manaqeb Ibn Shahr Ashoub V2 P262. Bishart Al-Mostafa P215. Tarikh Al-Damesh V3 P72. Nafahato Al-Lahout P114. Arjah Al-Mataleb P162. Maqsad Al-Ragheb P29. Majmaa Al-Zawaed V5 P185. Ibn Katheer in his tafseer V9 P200.

O Ali, on the Day of Judgement, you will be brought sitting on a MINBAR (chair) of light. There will be a crown on your head that shines so brightly that it will almost blind people.

God will call out, "Where is the successor of Mohammad, the Messenger of Allah?"

Then, O Ali, you will say, "Here I am."

Then the caller will say, "Those who loved you [Ali], let them enter Paradise, and those who were against you, send them to Hell."

Therefore, you (Ali﷽) will divide those who go to Paradise and those who go to Hell, and this is an order from the All-Powerful King.[16]

Virtue #12

Abu Mohammad Jaafar bin Ahmad bin Al-Husain Al-Shashi narrated from Ahmad bin Ziad Al-Qatan, from Yahya bin Abi Taleb, from Amr bin Abdul Ghaffar, from Aamash, from Abi Saleh, from Abu Huraira, who said:

I was with the Prophet﷽ when Ali bin Abi Taleb﷽ entered. The Prophet﷽ asked me, "O Abu Huraira, do you know who this is?"

I said, "Yes, O Messenger of God. This is Ali bin Abi Taleb﷽."

Then the Prophet﷽ said, "This (Ali﷽) is a sea full of treasures. He is the rising sun. He is more generous and giving than the river of Euphrates[17], and his heart is larger than the entire world. May God's curse be on those who hate him."[18]

Virtue #13

Abul Qassem Jaafar bin Mohammad bin Masrur narrated from Husain bin Mohammad, from Ahmad bin Alwea, known as Ibn Al-Aswad Al-Asbahani,

---

[16] Ghayatol Maram P69 H15. Sadough in Amal P295 H14. Bihar V7 P232. Jawahir Al-Sanniya P277. Ithbato Al-Hodat V3 P402. Tabari in Bishara P68. Qondouzi in Yanabi' Al-Mawaddah P83
[17] Note from Translator: River, sea, and water are used to express unlimited generosity in the Arabic language. Euphrates was commonly used as an example of a large river/sea.
[18] Kanz Al-Ommal P62. Bihar V27 P227 H29.

from Ibrahim bin Mohammad, from Abdullah bin Saleh, from Jarir bin Abdul Hamid, from Mujahed, from Ibn Abbas, who said:

I heard the Messenger of God ﷺ say:

On the night of Meraj, every time I passed by a group of angels they asked me about Ali bin Abi Taleb so often that I started to believe that Ali was more famous in the skies than I was.

When I reached the fourth sky, I saw the angel of death.

The angel of death asked me, "O Mohammad, how is Ali?"

I said, "O my friend, how do you know Ali?"

He said, "O Mohammad, I am responsible for taking the life of everyone that God has created except for two beings, that is, your life and Ali's life, because God himself will take your lives."

Then I reached under ARSH (the throne) and when I looked up there was Ali bin Abi Taleb standing under God's throne.

I said, "O Ali, did you race me up here?"

Then Jibraeel asked me, "O Mohammad, to whom are you speaking?"

I replied, "I am talking to my brother, Ali bin Abi Taleb."

Jibraeel replied, "O Mohammad, this is not Ali himself. This is an angel that God has created in the shape of Ali bin Abi Taleb. When we (angels) miss Ali bin Abi Taleb, we go and look at this angel and seek forgiveness from God for Ali's Shia."[19]

Virtue #14

Abul Hasan Ali bin Ahmad bin Motoeh Al-Makri narrated from Ahmad bin Mohammad, from Mohammad bin Ali, from Ali bin Uthman, from Mohammad bin Furat, from Mohammad bin Ali Al-Baqir ﷺ (5th Imam), from his father (4th Imam ﷺ), from his grandfather, Husain bin Ali ﷺ, from his father (Imam Ali ﷺ), who said:

The Messenger of God ﷺ said:

---

[19] Madinatol Maajiz P143 H404. Kanz Al-Ommal 259. Bihar V18 P300 H3

Ali bin Abi Taleb is God's successor and my successor.
He is God's decisive argument and he is my decisive argument. He is God's
door (the route to God) and he is my door (the route to me). He is God's
chosen one and my chosen one. God loves him and I love him. He is God's
love and he is my love. He is God's sword and my sword. He is my brother,
my companion, my minister, and my guardian. Those who love him love me,
and those who hate him hate me. His friends are my friends, and his
enemies are my enemies. He is my daughter's husband and his sons are my
sons. His war is my war. His words are my words. His orders are my orders.
He is the master of all the successors of the prophets. He is the best of my
nation. He is the master of all the people after me.[20]

Virtue #15

The judge, Al-Moaafi bin Zakariyya, narrated from Hasan bin Ali Al-Asemi,
from Suhaib, from his father, from Jaafar bin Mohammad Al-Sadiq, from
his father (5th Imam) from Ali bin Husain, from his father, Husain bin
Ali bin Abi Taleb, who said:

The Prophet was in Um Salama's house when an angel, who had twenty
heads, descended upon him. Each one of the angel's heads had one
thousand tongues, and he was praising God with each tongue in a different
language. His wings were larger than all of the seven heavens and the seven
earths.

The Prophet thought that he was Jibraeel so the Prophet said to
him, "I have never seen you in this form."

The angel said, "I am not Jibraeel. I am Sarsaeel. God sent me to you to
marry the light to the light."

Then the Prophet asked him, "Who do you mean?"

The angel said, "Your daughter, Fatema, to Ali bin Abi Taleb."

So the Prophet married Fatema to Ali with Jibraeel, Mikaeel,
Israfil, and Sarsaeel as witnesses.

Then the Prophet looked and saw the following written between the
shoulders of Sarsaeel:

---

[20] Ghayatol Maram P69 H16. Kanz Al-Ommal 185. Ithbat Al-Hodat V3 P632 H860. Bihar V26 P263 H47

LA ILAHA ILLALLAH. MOHAMMAD IS THE MESSENGER OF GOD AND IS THE PROPHET WHO BRINGS MERCY ON PEOPLE. ALI IS THE DECISIVE ARGUMENT THAT GOD USES ON HIS CREATURES.

Then the Prophetﷺ asked Sarsaeel, "How long have you had this written between your shoulders?"

Sarsaeel replied, "Twelve thousand years before God created Adam."[21]

Virtue #16

Abu Abdullah Mohammad bin Wahban Al-Hinad narrated from Ahmad bin Ibrahim, from Husain bin Abdullah Al-Zafrani, from Ibrahim bin Mohammad Al-Thaqafi, from Yahya bin Abdul Quddous, from Ali bin Mohammad Al-Taialisi, from Mohammad bin Wakee Al-Jarrah, from Fadeel bin Marzouq, from Atiya Al-Owfai, from Abi Saeed Al-Khodri, who said:

I heard the Messenger of Godﷺ say:

When the Day of Judgement comes, God will order two angels to sit down at the SIRAT' (bridge) and guard it. No one will be able to cross the bridge without having a pass issued by Ali bin Abi Taleb. God will order the two angels to stop those who do not have a pass and ask them about it. If they fail to answer, these angels will throw them into Hell, head first.

The Prophetﷺ then referred to this verse from the Qur'an as evidence, "And stop them, for verily they must be questioned" (37:24).

Then I asked the Prophetﷺ, "O the Messenger of God, may I ransom my father and my mother for you. Please tell me what this pass is?"

The Prophetﷺ replied, "This is what is written on the pass with a very bright light:

LA ILAHA ILLALLAH.
MOHAMMADUN RASULULLAH.
ALIYUN WALIYULLAH.[22]

---

[21] Madinatol Majiz P158 H463. Kharazmi in Manaqeb P245. Kashf Al-Ghomma V1 P352. Bihar V43 P123 H31. Mohtazar P133.
[22] Yaghin fi Imrat amir al Momenin P57. Borhan V4 P17 H3. Ghayatol Maram P17 H10. Bihar V39 P201 H22

Virtue #17

Ahmad bin Mohammad bin Ubaidullah Al-Hafiz narrated from Ali bin Sinan Al-Mawsili, from Ahmad bin Mohammad Al-Khalili Al-Amali, from Mohammad bin Saleh, from Suleiman bin Ahmad, from Ziad bin Muslim, from Abdul Rahman bin Yazid bin Jabir, from Salam from Abi Salma, who said:

I heard the Messenger of God ﷺ say:

On the night of Meraj God asked me, "Did the Messenger believe in what was revealed to him from his Lord?"

I said, "Yes. And the believers believed in Allah, His angels, His books, and His messengers."

God said: "You are right."

Then God asked, "Who did you choose as a successor?"

I said, "The best of my nation."

God asked, "Do you mean Ali bin Abi Taleb?"

I replied, "Yes, O Allah!"

Then God said:

O Mohammad, I looked at all of My creation and I chose you from among all of them. Then I derived a name for you from My name. Therefore, it is not permitted that anyone mention Me without mentioning you with Me. My name is Mahmoud and your name is Mohammad. Then I looked again [at all of My creation] and I chose Ali, and I derived a name for him from My name. So My name is Ali, the extremely high, and his name is Ali. O Mohammad, I created you, Ali, Fatema, Hasan, Husain, and the rest of the Imams from Husain's sons from My own light. Then I asked all of my creation in the skies and the earths to accept your WILAYAT. I consider those who accept it as believers, and I consider those who refuse it as KAFERS.

O Mohammad, if a slave from among My slaves worships Me until he is torn and nothing is left from him, but he refuses to accept your WILAYAT, Ali's WILAYAT, and the WILAYAT of the Imams from his sons, I will not accept him or forgive him until he accepts your WILAYAT, Ali's WILAYAT, and the WILAYAT of the Imams from his sons.

Then God asked me, "O Mohammad, would you like to see them?"

I replied, "Yes, O Allah."

God said, "Look to the right of the throne."

Then I looked and I saw Ali, Fatema, Hasan, Husain, Ali bin Husain, Mohammad bin Ali, Jaafar bin Mohammad, Musa bin Jaafar, Ali bin Musa, Mohammad bin Ali, Ali bin Mohammad, Hasan bin Ali, and the Mahdi. They were surrounded by light and were all standing and praying to God. Mahdi was in the center and he was shining like a brilliant star.

Then God said:

> O Mohammad, they are My decisive arguments, and Mahdi will take revenge on My behalf. I swear by My Magnificence, he supports My friends and takes revenge on My enemies. Following them and accepting their WILAYAT is WAJIB (obligatory) on everyone. With my permission, they prevent the skies from falling on the earth.[23]

Virtue #18

Mohammad bin Saeed Abul Faraj narrated from Ahmad bin Mohammad bin Saeed, from Saad bin Turayf Al-Khaffaf, from Saeed bin Jubair, from Ibn Abbas, who said:

The Messenger of God said to Ali:

O Ali, I am the city of knowledge and you are its door. The city can only be entered through its door.

Those who claim that they love me but hate you are lying because you are from me and I am from you; your flesh is my flesh; your blood is my blood; your soul is from my soul; what you hide is what I hide; and what you show is what I show.

You are the Imam of my nation and my successor.

Those who obey you succeed, and those who disobey you fail. Those who follow you will benefit, and those who are against you will lose. Those who are committed to you are winners, and those who abandon you are losers.

---

[23] Bihar v27 p199 h27. Madinatol Maajiz p143 h405. Arbaeen Khatoon Al-Abadi h17. Kharazmi in Maqtal v1 p95. Taraaef p170 h270. Helyatol Abrar v2 p720. Yanabee Al-Mawaddah p486. Sirat Al-Mostaqim v2 p117. Ghayatol Maram p35 h21. Elzam Al-Nasseb v1 p186. Faraed Al-Semtain v2 319 h 571. Tousi in Al-Ghaybah p95. Ethbatol Hodat v2 p462. Forat Al-Koufi in his tafsir p 5.

You and the Imams after you are like the ark of Nuh. The riders of the ark survived, and those who stayed behind drowned.

You are like the stars. Whenever one star disappears, another one appears until the Day of Judgement.[24]

Virtue #19

Mohammad bin Hamid Al-Jarrar narrated from Hasan bin Abdul Samad, from Yahya bin Mohammad bin Qassem Al-Qazwini, from Mohammad bin Hasan Al-Hafiz, from Ahmad bin Mohammad, from Hadba bin Khaled, from Hammad bin Salma, from Thabit, from Anas bin Malik[25], who said:

God created seventy thousand angels from the light of Ali's face. All they do is seek forgiveness for him[26], for his Shia, and for those who love him until the Day of Judgement.[27]

---

[24] Ghayatol Maram p543. Sadough in Amalih p222. Kamalo Al-Deen v1 p241. Bihar v23 p125 h53. Tabari in Besharatol Mostafa p39. Faraet Al-Semtain v2 p243. Jameol Al-Akhbar p16. Bihar v40 p 203 h9. Khatib in Tarikh Al-Baghdad v11 p204. Asqalani in Lisan Al-Mizan v5 p19.

[25] Note from Translator: "Anas" was well-respected and trusted because he was a servant of the Prophet. Therefore, the reader will see his name in many AHADITH in this book. The Prophet made sure that Anas heard him talking about Imam Ali and kept warning Anas of the day on which his testimony would be required. After the Prophet died, Imam Ali, in his argument with Abu Bakr, asked Anas to testify and tell people some of the AHADITH that he had heard from the Prophet. Anas refused, saying that he had become old and that he did not remember anything. Imam Ali told him, "If you lie I will curse you." However, Anas insisted that he did not remember anything, so Imam Ali cursed him in front of all of people in the Prophet's mosque. Anas was blinded instantly and became ill with a disease that ate his skin until he died.

[26] Note from Translator: The Commander of the Believers, Fatema, Master of the Worlds Women, and their eleven sons, the Imams, are infallible just as the Messenger of God, according to the following verses in the Qur'an: AHZAB:33, ALI IMRAN: 61, AN NISA: 59, AT TAWBAH:119, MA-IDAH:55, RA'D:43, HAJJ:77-78, NAHL:43, ANBIYA:73, SAJDAH:24, NUR:55.

The fact that angels seek forgiveness for the Commander of the Believers is just like the fact that God tells His Messenger in the Qur'an, "So that Allah may forgive your sins and that which is to come" (48:2).

Mofadhhal asked Imam Al-Sadiq, "What were the sins of the Prophet that God forgave?" The Imam replied, "The Messenger of God had no sins but he asked God to make him accountable for all of the sins of his Shia, the Shia of Ali, and the Shia of the Imams from his sons until the Day of Judgement. The Prophet also asked God not to expose the sins of the Shia (for which he accepted to be accountable) in front of the other prophets. So God revealed this

14

Virtue #20

Sahl bin Ahmad bin Abdullah narrated from Mohammad bin Jarir, from
Hasan bin Ibrahim Al-Baghdadi, from Mohammad bin Yacoub Al-Imam, from
Ahmad Ibn Yahya, from Abdul Rahman Al-Mahdi, from Ibn Abbas, who said:

A man came to the Prophet ﷺ and asked him, "Will I benefit from the love
of Ali bin Abi Taleb ؏?"

The Prophet ﷺ replied, "I do not know until I ask Jibraeel."

So Jibraeel came to the Prophet ﷺ immediately. The Prophet ﷺ asked
him [the above question].

Jibraeel replied, "I do not know. I have to ask Israfil."

So Jibraeel went up and asked Israfil, "Will the love for Ali ؏ benefit
anyone?"

Israfil replied, "I do not know until I speak to my Magnificent Lord."

Then God sent the following revelation to Israfil:

> Tell those angels trustworthy of My revelation to send My greetings
> to My love, Mohammad, and tell him that God sends His salaam, and
> tells you that, 'You are as close to Me as I want you to be. And Ali and
> I are as close to you as you are to Me. And those who love Ali are as
> close to Me as Ali is to you.'[28]

Virtue #21

Hasan bin Hamza bin Abdullah narrated from Ahmad bin Al-Hasan Al-
Khashab, from Ayyoub bin Nuh, from Abbas, from Amro bin Aban, from Aban
bin Taqlab, from Akrama, from Ibn Abbas, who said:

After returning from the farewell pilgrimage, the Messenger of God ﷺ
said:

---

verse to him which means God forgave the sins of Shia." Anwar Al-No'maniyya V2 P92, Tafsir Al-
Qummi V2 P314

[27] Ghayatol Maram P585 H75. Madinatol Maajez P173 H487. Kharazmi in Manaqeb P31. Kharazmi
in Maqtal Al-Husain V1 P39. Misbah Al-Anwar P64. Ershal Al-Qoloub P234. Ghayatol Maram P8
H18. Manaqeb Al-Mortazawiyyah p220. Kashf Al-ghomma V1 P103. Bihar Al-Anwar V39 P275 H52.

[28] Ghayatol Maram P585 H76. Madinatol Maajez P163 H450. Jawaher Al-Saniyyah

O people! Jibraeel, the Honest Spirit, came to me from God, the Magnificent, and said, "O Mohammad, Allah says that he misses seeing you. So prepare a good will and finish what you have to do."

O people! My time has come and I can see us leaving one another. So if your bodies have left me, do not allow your souls to do the same.

O people! God has never created an immortal prophet, and I am not immortal. God has said in this verse in the Qur'an, "We have not granted to any man before you eternal life. What! If you die, will they live for ever? Every soul shall taste of death" (21:34-35). Understand that my Lord has ordered me to leave a will for you.

Understand that my Lord has ordered me to show you to the ark of rescue and the door of sustenance. Those of you who want to survive after me and be safe from the destroying seductions should hold firmly to the WILAYAT (command) of Ali bin Abi Taleb. He is the most truthful and the best separator of right from wrong.

He is the IMAM of every Muslim after me.

Those who love him and follow him will be next to me by the Pool of Kawthar on the Day of Judgement. I will see those who disobey him on the Day of Judgement, but they will not see me. They will be pulled towards others who will take them deep into Hell.

Then the Prophetﷺ said, "O people! I have given you the best advice but you do not like the advisors. I say this and I seek forgiveness for myself and for you." Then he held Ali's head and kissed his forehead.[29]

Then the Prophetﷺ said to Ali, "O Ali, your high qualities cannot be counted. I swear to God, who created the seeds and created people, if all creatures would concede to loving you and understanding your true status, God would not have created Hell."[30]

Virtue #22

Abul Qassem Jaafar bin Mohammad Al-Qulieh narrated from Ali bin Husain, from Ali bin Ibrahim, from his father, from Ahmad bin Mohammad, from Mohammad bin Fudail, from Thabet bin Abi Hamza, from Ali bin Al-Husain

---

[29] Note from Translator: Kissing the forehead is a sign of extreme respect among the Arabs.
[30] Ghayatol Maram P45 H48. Ehqaq Al-Haq V4 P331.

16

(4th Imam), from his father (Imam Husain), from the Commander of the Believers , who said:

The Messenger of God said:

God has decreed you to follow my command and he has forbidden you from disobeying me. He has made it WAJIB on you to follow my orders and to obey Ali bin Abi Taleb after me.

He is my brother, my minister, and he inherits all of my knowledge.

He is from me and I am from him. Loving him is IMAN (faith) and hating him is KUFR (disbelief). Beware! Of whomsoever I am their MOWLA (Master), Ali is their MOWLA.

Ali and I are the fathers of this nation. Those who disobey their fathers will be gathered with Nuh's son on the Day of Judgement. Nuh told his son, "O son ride with us and don't be from the KAFERS. [His son replied] I will resort to a mountain" (11:42-43).

Then the Prophet said, "O Allah, support those who support Ali; disappoint those who disappoint him; befriend his friends, and be the enemy of his enemies."

Then the Prophet started to cry. The Muhajerin (Immigrants of Makkah) and Ansar (Supporters from Medina) who were sitting around him all cried. After that, three groups of people (from among the Muhajerin and Ansar) stood up and bade farewell to the Prophet .[31]

Virtue #23

Ahmad bin Mohammad narrated from his book, from Abdullah bin Jaafar, from Ibrahim bin Hashem, from Jaafar bin Mohammad bin Marwan, from his father, from Ubaidullah bin Yahya, from Mohammad bin Ali Al-Baqir (5th Imam), from his father, from Husain bin Ali , from the Commander of the Believers , who said:

The Messenger of God said the following about this verse, "Cast you two every ingrate rebel into Hell" (50:24).

---

[31] Ghayatol Maram P165 H51. Kanz Al-Ommal P185. Bihar Al-Anwar V26 P263 H48. Ethbat Al-Hodat V3 P379 H218. Rowzat Al-Jannat V6 P184. Sadough in Amali P22 H6. Tabari in Besharatol Mustafa P196.

O Ali, on the Day of Judgement, when God gathers all the creatures in the same desert, you and I will be on the right side of God's throne and God will say, "O Mohammad and Ali, stand up and throw those who hated you[32], did not believe you, and disobeyed you into Hell."[33]

Virtue #24

Mohammad bin Abdullah bin Ubaid narrated from Mohammad bin Qassem, from Ibad bin Yacoub, from Amro bin Abi Al-Meqdam, from his father, from Saeed bin Jubair, from Ibn Abbas, who said:

The Messenger of God﷽ said:

I swear to God, who has sent me as a Warner and a guide, that the throne of God did not settle, the universes did not start moving, and the heavens and the planets were not created until after God wrote on them:

LA ILAHA ILLALLAH.
MOHAMMADUN RASULLULLAH.
ALIYUN WALIYULLAH.

Then the Prophet﷽ explained what God told him, in His own voice:

God said, "O Mohammed"

I replied, "LABBAYK WA SAADAYK."

God said:

> I am Mahmoud and you are Mohammad. I derived your name from mine and I made you superior to all of My creatures. Assign your brother, Ali, to be a flag for My slaves to guide them to My religion.
>
> O Mohammad, I have made the believers the chosen ones, and I have made Ali their commander. Therefore, I curse those who give commands to Ali and I torture those who disobey him. But those who follow him, I will bring them closer to Me.

---

[32] Note from Translator: God has grouped those who hate Imam Ali with those who hate the Prophet in the same group. This means it is not possible to love the Prophet and hate Imam Ali!

[33] Ghayatol Maram P390 S101 H2. Borhan V4 P227 H18. Lawamee Al-Nawraniyyah P409. Tafsir Al-Qommi P644. Bihar Al-Anwar V39 P199 H13. Tafseer Forat A-Koufi P166 and 167. Shawahid Al-Tanzil V2 P191 H897. Manaqeb Ibn Shar Ahoub V2 P8. Yanbee Al-Mawaddah P85.

O Mohammad, I have made Ali the Imam of Muslims, Those who proclaim to precede him, I disgrace them. I imprison those who disobey him.

I have made Ali the master of all of the successors, and I have made him the glorified leader of the believers.

He is My decisive argument on My entire creation.[34]

Virtue #25

Ahmad bin Mohammad bin Imran narrated from Hasan bin Mohammad Al-Askari, from Ibrahim bin Ubaidullah, from Abdul Razzaq, from Mo'ammar, from Yahya bin Abi Katheer, from his father, from Abu Harun Al-Abdi, from Jabir bin Abdullah Al-Ansari, who said:

The Messenger of God 🕌 said the following about Ali bin Abi Taleb 👤:

> He was the first one to believe in Islam;
> He is the most knowledgeable;
> He is the most correct one in his DEEN (religion);
> He is the most certain;
> He is the most patient;
> He is the most forgiving and generous;
> He is the most brave;
> He is the IMAM and the successor after me.[35]

Virtue #26

Sahl bin Ahmad bin Abdullah narrated from Ali bin Abdullah, from Ishaq bin Ibrahim Al-Debri, from Abdul Razzaq bin Hamam, from Mo'ammar, from Abdullah bin Tawus, from his father, from Ibn Abbas, who said:

We were sitting with the Prophet 🕌 when Ali bin Abi Taleb 👤 entered.

Ali 👤 said, "ASSALAMO ALAIKA, O Messenger of God."

The Prophet 🕌 replied, "WA ALAIK ASSALAAM, O Commander of the Believers."

---

[34] Al-Yaqeen fi Emrat Amir Al Momenin P57. Madinatol Maajez P157 H428. Ghayatol Maram P17 H11. Bihar Al-Anwar V27 P8 H16. Jawaher Al-Saniyyah P300. Taweel Al-Ayat P186 H34.
[35] Ghayatol Maram P45 H51. Kanz Al-Ommal P121. Ethbat Al-Hodat V3 P633 H862. Sadough in Amali P16 H6. Bihar Al-Anwar V38 P90 H1. Helyato Abrar V1 P235.

Ali responded, "O Prophet, you call me the Commander of Believers while you are still alive?"

The Prophet answered, "Yes, while I am alive."

Then the Prophet continued, "O Ali, you passed by Jibraeel and I yesterday and did not say salaam. So Jibraeel said, 'Why did the Commander of the Believers not say salaam to us. I swear to God, we would have been pleased if he had said salaam to us and we would have responded."

Ali answered, "It looked like you and Dehya[36] were in a private meeting so I did not want to interrupt."

The Prophet said, "He was not Dehya, he was Jibraeel. I asked Jibraeel why he called you the Commander of the Believers. Jibraeel told me that in the Battle of Badr, God told Jibraeel to come to me (the Prophet) and tell me to order the Commander of the Believers to ride his horse in front of the army lines because the angels love to watch him do that. So God named you the Commander of the Believers that day in the heavens."

Then the Prophet said, "O Ali, you are the commander of everyone in the heavens and the commander of everyone on earth. You are the commander of those who have passed away and the commander of those who are yet to come. There is no commander before you and no commander after you. It is forbidden for anyone who has not received this title from God to be called by this name."[37]

Virtue #27

Mohammad bin Abdullah bin Abi Ubaidullah Al-Shaibani narrated from Mohammad bin Yahya Al-Tameemi, from Abu Qotada Al-Harrani, from his father, from Hareth bin Al-Khazraj, the holder of the flag of Ansar (supporters of Medina), who said:

---

[36] Note from translator: "Dehya Al-Kalbi" was one the companions of the Prophet. He was raised by the Prophet and he was very handsome. It was very common for Angel Jibraeel to come down to Prophet in the form of Dehya. When Jibraeel would appear as Dehya, people could see and hear him, mainly because the Prophet wanted them to hear what Jibraeel was saying. The Prophet had ordered his companions not to approach him when they saw him alone with Dehya.

[37] Al-Yaqeen P58 S79. Ghayatol Maram P18 H12. Madinatol Maajez P8. Sirath AL-Mostaqim V2 P54. Bihar Al-Anwar V37 P307 H39. Manaqeb Ibn Shar Ahoub V2 P253.

I heard the Messenger of God ﷺ telling Ali bin Abi Taleb ؑ:

No one precedes you after me except a KAFER, and no one disobeys you except a KAFER. The people of the seven skies call you the Commander of the Believers by the order of God.[38]

Virtue #28

My father narrated from Mohammad bin Husain, from Mohammad bin Hasan Al-Saffar, from Ahmad bin Mohammad, from his father, from Abdullah bin Al-Moghira and Mohammad bin Yahya Al-Khothami, from Mohammad bin Bohloul Al-Abdi, from Jaafar bin Mohammad ؑ (Imam Al-Sadiq), from his father, Mohammad bin Ali ؑ, from his father (4th Imam ؑ), from his father, Husain bin Ali ؑ, who said:

The Messenger of God ﷺ said that on the night of Meraj when he went up and passed the gates of light, God talked to him, and said:

> O Mohammad, convey My salaam to Ali bin Abi Taleb, and inform him that he is My decisive argument on all creatures after you. I pour the rain of My blessings on My slaves through him; I keep everything evil away from them through him; and he is My decisive argument on them when they meet Me.
>
> So they should follow his commands, obey his orders, and abstain when he abstains. If they do, I will sit them next to Me and I will allow them to enter My Paradise. If they do not, I will put them with the worst of My enemies in Hell and I will not care.[39]

Virtue #29

Sahl bin Ahmad Al-Taraeqi and Mohammad bin Abdullah Al-Kufi narrated from Mohammad bin Jarir Al-Tabari, from Khalaf bin Khalifa, from Yazid bin Harun, from Mohammad bin Ibrahim bin Ibrahim bin Mubasher, from Jabir bin Abdullah Al-Ansari, who said:

I was sitting with the Prophet ﷺ when Ali bin Abi Taleb ؑ came. The Prophet ﷺ brought him close to him, and wiped his (Ali's ؑ) forehead

---

[38] Ghayatol Maram P69 H17. Al-Yaqeen P78. Misbah Al-Anwar P164. Ethbat Al-Hodat V4 P170 H517. Sirath Al-Mostaqeem V2 P55. Manaqeb Ibn Shar Ahoub V2 P254. Bihar Al-Anwar V37 P310 H43.
[39] Madinatol Maajez P157 H430. Tabari in Besharatol Mustafa P79. Bihar Al-Anwar V38 P138 H99

with his abaa and said to him, "O Abal Hasan, shall I tell you the good news that Jibraeel gave me?"

Ali ﷺ replied, "Yes, O Messenger of God."

The Prophet ﷺ said,

> There is a well in Paradise called "Tasneem." Two rivers emerge from it and (they are so large that) all of the ships of the world can sail on them.

> There are several trees on the shores of "Tasneem." Their branches are pearls and coral, and the grass there is saffron. Directly adjacent to the trees, there are people sitting on chairs made of light on whose foreheads, written in light, is 'These are the believers; these are the lovers of Ali bin Abi Taleb.'[40]

Virtue #30

Ahmad bin Mohammad bin Abdullah bin Ayyash Al-Hafez narrated from the judge, Abdul Baqi bin Falea, from Husain bin Mohammad, from Suleiman bin Qarm, from Mohammad bin Shaiba, from Dawud bin Ali, from his father, from his grandfather, Abdullah bin Abbas, who said:

The Messenger of God ﷺ said to Ali bin Abi Taleb ﷺ:

O Ali, Jibraeel said something about you that made me extremely happy and pleased me.

He (Jibraeel) said:

> O Mohammad, Allah told me to convey His salaam to you and to tell you that Ali is the Imam of Guidance; he is the light in darkness; and he is My decisive argument on the people of the world.

> He is the most truthful and the greatest separator of right from wrong.

> I forbid Myself to allow those who love him, follow him, and follow the Imams after him, to enter Hell. I forbid Myself to allow those who do not accept his command and do not follow him and the Imams after him to enter Paradise.

---

[40] Borhan V4 P440 H10. Ghayatol Maram P586 H78.

I have most certainly committed to fill Hell with his enemies from among the people and the jinn, and to fill Paradise with his Shia and friends from among My creatures.[41]

Virtue #31

Mohammad bin Hammad bin Bashir narrated from Mohammad bin Hasan bin Abdul Karim, from Ibrahim bin Maimun and Uthman bin Saeed, from Abdul Karim bin Yaqoub, from Diya Al-Jaafi, from Abi Tufail, from Anas bin Malik, who said:

I (Anas bin Malek) was the servant of the Prophetﷺ. Once while I was helping the Prophetﷺ do his WUDHU (ablution), the Prophetﷺ said, "The person who will enter just now is the Commander of the Believers, the Master of Muslims, and the best of successors. He is worthy of having a higher authority on people than they have on themselves, and he is the glorified leader of those who seek God."

"O God, make it someone from the Ansar (supporters of Medina)," I (Anas bin Malek) prayed to myself.

Then someone knocked at the door. It was Ali bin Abi Talebﷺ.

When Aliﷺ entered, the Prophet'sﷺ face started to sweat profusely. The Prophetﷺ wiped the sweat from his face and put it over Ali'sﷺ face.

"Did you receive a revelation?" Aliﷺ asked (the Prophetﷺ)

The Messenger of Godﷺ said, "You are from me; you repay my debt; you perform my religious affairs; you will clear my liabilities; and you will preach my prophethood," the Prophetﷺ replied.

"Did you not preach it yourself?" Aliﷺ asked.

"Yes I did, but people need to learn the TA'WIL (deeper, inner meaning) of Qur'an after me, and you will teach them things that they did not learn during my time," the Prophetﷺ replied.[42]

---

[41] Bihar Al-Anwar V37 P113 H88. Ghayatol Maram P45 H52.
[42] Al-Yaqeen P59. Ghayatol Maram P18 H3. Bihar Al-Anwar V37 P296 H13. Al-Mostadrak V3 P192 H32. Manaqeb Ibn Shar Ahoub V2 P253.

Virtue #32

Abu Abdullah Mohammad bin Ali bin Zangoeh narrated from Mohammad bin Jaafar, from Jaafar bin Salma, from Ibrahim bin Mohammad, from Abu Ghasan, from Yahya bin Salma, from his father, from Abi Edris, from Mosayyeb, from the Commander of the Believers, who said:

I swear to God that the Messenger of God made me the successor of his nation. Therefore, I am God's decisive argument after the Prophet, and I swear that following me is mandatory on the inhabitants of the heavens as it is on the inhabitants of earth. When angels want to praise God they talk about my qualities.

O people! Follow me and I will guide you to the path of righteousness. Do not go right or left because you will get lost. I am the heir of your Prophet and his successor. I am the Imam of the pious and the believers; I am their commander and their Master. I will lead my Shia to Paradise and my enemies to Hell.

I am God's sword on His enemies and I am His mercy on His friends.

I am the owner of the Prophet's Pool (Pool of Kawthar) and I carry his flag.

I have his position and I have his right of intercession.

Me and Hasan, Husain, the nine sons of Husain, are God's successors in His land. We are the only ones trustworthy of His revelation. We are the Imams of Muslims after the Prophet and we are God's decisive arguments on His creatures.[43]

Virtue #33

Mohammad bin Saeed Al-Dehqan narrated from Mohammad bin Masoud, from Ahmad bin Isa Al-Alwy, from Husain from Abi Khaled and Zaid bin Ali, from his father (4th Imam), from his grandfather, Husain bin Ali (3rd Imam), from the Commander of the Believers, who said:

I [Imam Ali] went to the Prophet when he was in one of his houses. I asked his permission to enter and he granted it.

---

[43] Ghayatol Maram P18 H14.

When I entered, the Prophetﷺ asked me, "O Ali, do you not know that my house is your house? Why do you seek permission to enter?"

I replied, "I like to do that."

The Prophetﷺ said:

> You like what God likes and you use His manners. O Ali, do you not know that you are my brother, and my Creator did not want me to have a brother other than you. O Ali, you are my heir, and you will be oppressed and wronged after my death. O Ali, those who are devoted to following you are like those who live with me (in my place in Paradise), and those who abandon you, abandon me. O Ali, those who think that they love me but hate you, lie because God created you and I from the same light.[44]

Virtue #34

Ahmad bin Mohammad narrated from Mohammad bin Jaafar, from Mohammad bin Husain, from Mohammad bin Sinan, from Ziad bin Munzer, from Saeed bin Jubair, from Ibn Abbas, who said:

The Messenger of Godﷺ said:

No one has a higher status than Ali bin Abi Taleb except me. He is the Imam of my nation; he is my heir; and he is my successor. Those who follow him are guided to the right path; those who follow anyone other than him (Aliﷺ) are lost and have strayed off the right path.

Indeed, I am the chosen Prophet. I do not say this about Ali from my own inclination. What I say is nothing but revelation brought by Jibraeel from God, who owns everything in the skies and in the earth, and whatever is between the skies and the earth, and whatever is under the earth.[45]

Virtue #35

Abul Tayyeb Mohammad bin Husain Al-Timali narrated from Motair bin Mohammad bin Abd, from Yahya Al-Jammal, from Hisham, from Abu Harun Al-Abdi, from Abi Saeed Al-Khodri, who said:

---

[44] Ghayatol Maram P7 H12. Al-Mostadrak V2 P71 H1. Kanz Al-Ommal P208. Bihar Al-Anwar V27 P230 H38. Rowzat Al-Jannat V6 P184.
[45] Ghayatol Maram P45 H54. Kanz Al-Ommal P208. Bihar Al-Anwar V25 P361 H31. Ethbat Al-Hodat V3 P633 H864. Rowzat Al-Jannat V6 P185

The Messenger of God 卌 said:

On the night of Meraj, I did not pass through any of the skies or any of its layers without finding it filled with noble angels calling me and saying:

> O Mohammad, enjoy what God gave no one before you and no one after you. You were given Ali bin Abi Taleb as a brother; Fatema, his wife, as a daughter; Hasan and Husain as sons; and their lovers, as your Shia.

> O Mohammad, you are the best of the prophets; Ali is the best of successors; Fatema is the Master of all the Worlds' Women; Hasan and Husain are the most respected of all of those who enter Paradise; and their Shia are the best of people on the Day of Judgement. They (their Shia) will gather in the rooms of Paradise, its palaces, and its parks.

The angels continued saying this while I was going up until I came back down. If it was not for God preventing this from being heard, everyone, from among the people and the Jinn, would have heard it.[46]

Virtue #36

Mohammad bin Mohammad bin Murra narrated from Hasan bin Ali Al-Asemi, from Mohammad bin Abdul Malik bin Abi Al-Shawareb, from Jaafar bin Suleiman Al-Dabei, from Saad bin Zarif, from Asbagh, who said:

Salman Al-Farsi was asked about the status of Ali bin Abi Taleb 卌 and Fatema 卌.

So Salman Al-Farsi said that he heard the Prophet 卌 say:

> Pay attention to Ali 卌 because he is your master, so love him. He is the most respected, so follow him. He is the most knowledgeable among you, so honour him. He is your leader to Paradise, so reward him.

> When he calls you, answer his call. When he orders you, obey him. Love him for me and respect him for me.

> I did not say any of this about Ali 卌 without an order from God, the Great.

---

[46] Ghayatol Maram P166 H56.

Virtue #37

Abu Bakr Mohammad bin Ahmad bin Ghatrif Al-Jorjani narrated from Abu Khalifa Fadl bin Saleh Al-Gahmi, from Ali bin Abdullah bin Jaafar, from Mohammad bin Ubaid, from Abdullah, from Nafi', from Abdullah, son of Omar, from Omar bin Al-Khattab, who said:

We asked the Messenger of God ﷺ about Ali bin Abi Taleb's ؏ status. The Prophet ﷺ got angry and said:

What is wrong with you people, asking me about someone to whom God has given a rank and position as high as mine, except for the prophethood?!

Beware! Those who love Ali love me, and those who love me please God, and God rewards them with Paradise.

Beware! The angels seek forgiveness for those who love Ali. The gates of Paradise are open for them, and they will enter from any door they choose without being questioned.

Beware! God will give those who love Ali their book [of deeds] in their right hand, and their questioning [on the Day of Judgement] is an easy questioning; it is like the questioning of the prophets.

Beware! Those who love Ali will not leave this world without first drinking from the Pool of Kawthar, eating from the tree of TOUBA, and seeing their place in Paradise.

Beware! God eases the death process of those who love Ali, and makes their graves a garden from the gardens of Paradise.

Beware! God gives those who love Ali one HUR, for each vein in their body. They (those who love Ali) will intercede for eighty of their family members and God will give them one city in Paradise for every hair on their body.

Beware! God sends the angel of death to those who know and love Ali in the same way He does to the prophets. He removes the terror of Munkar and Nakeer; He lights their graves and makes it (their graves) as big as seventy light years; and He raises them on the Day of Judgement with their faces shining brightly.

Beware! God places those who love Ali under the shade of His throne with the company of the truthful, the martyrs, and the virtuous. They are safe from the great and the loud terrors on the Day of Judgement.

Beware! The good deeds of those who love Ali are accepted and their sins are forgiven. They will be in Paradise in the company of Hamza (the Prophet's uncle), the Master of the Martyrs.

Beware! God places wisdom in the hearts of those who love Ali; God places truth on their tongues; and God opens the doors of His mercy to them.

Beware! Earth is the prison of those who love Ali and God will free them. Allah boasts about them to His angels and to those who carry His throne.

Beware! An angel will call on those who love Ali from under God's throne and say, "O Allah's servant, carry on because all of your sins are forgiven."

Beware! On the Day of Judgement the faces of those who love Ali will be shining like a full moon.

Beware! God will place the crown of dignity on the heads of those who love Ali and they will wear the suit of glory.

Beware! Those who love Ali will pass the bridge with the speed of light and will not feel the difficulty associated with passing.

Beware! God writes a guarantee (of protection) from Hell to those who love Ali, and a pass for the bridge and a guarantee (of protection) from the torture.

Beware! The book of those who love Ali will not be published and they (those who love Ali) will not be measured; they will be told to enter Paradise without judgement.

Beware! Those who love the family of the Prophet are secure from the calculation, the scale, and the bridge.

Beware! Angels shake hands with those who die with the love of the family of the Prophet. The souls of the prophets come to visit them and God fulfills all of their requests.

Beware! Those who die hating the family of the Prophet die as KAFER.

Beware! Those who die with the love of the family of the Prophet die with faith, and I guarantee Paradise for them.

Beware! Those who die hating the family of the Prophet will have the following written between their eyes on the Day of Judgement, "Excluded from the Mercy of God."

Beware! Those who die hating the family of the Prophet will not even smell the fragrance of Paradise.

Beware! Those who die hating the family of the Prophet will come out of their graves with black faces.[47]

Virtue #38

Ahmad bin Hasan bin Mohammad Al-Nishabori narrated in his book, from Mohammad bin Husain Al-Agri, from Jaafar bin Mohammad bin Al-E'zzi, from Qutaibah bin Saeed, from Jorair, from Moghira, from Mohammad bin Amro bin Abi Salma, from Ibn Abbas, who said:

The Messenger of God ﷺ said:

Ali to me is like my blood is to my body. Those who accept his authority are rightly guided. Those who love him are on the right path. Those who follow him are the survivors.

Beware that Ali is one of the four in Paradise, who are Hasan, Husain, Ali, and myself.[48]

Virtue #39

Al-Sharif Hasan bin Hamza Al-Alawy narrated from Ubaidullah bin Musa, from Al-Zohari, from Urwah, from Ibn Abbas, who said:

The Messenger of God ﷺ said:

Shaking hands with Ali is exactly like shaking hands with me, and shaking hands with me is like shaking hands with the corners of the throne of God.

Embracing Ali is exactly like embracing me, and embracing me is like embracing all of the prophets.

God forgives all of the sins of those who shake hands with those who love Ali and takes them to Paradise without judgement.[49]

---

[47] Bihar Al-Anwar V27 P114 H89. Ghayatol Maram P207 H10. Fazael Al-Shia P2 H1. Taawil Al-Ayyat P863 H1. Tabari in Besharatol Mustafa P36. Arbaeen Al-Khozayee H1.
[48] Ghayatol Maram P207 H11.
[49] Bihar Al-Anwar V27 P115 H90. Kharazmi in Manaqeb P226. Misbah Al-Anwar P122. Ghayatol Maram P583 H47.

Virtue #40

Sheikh Abu Abdullah Husain bin Abdullah Al-Qatiei narrated from Abul Hasan Mohammad bin Ahmad Al-Hashmi Al-Mansuri, from Abu Musa Isa bin Ahmad, from Ali bin Mohammad (10th Imam), from his father (9th Imam), from Ali bin Musa Al-Redha (8th Imam), from his father (7th Imam), from Jaafar bin Mohammad (6th Imam), from his father (5th Imam), from Ali bin Al-Husain (4th Imam), from his father, Imam Husain, from Qanbar (Imam Ali's servant), who said:

I was with the Commander of the Believers on the shore of the Euphrates River when he took his shirt off and entered the river. A large wave came and pulled his shirt into the water.

When the Commander of the Believers came out of the water, he was upset that he could not find his shirt.

Then a voice called to Ali and said, "O Abal Hasan, look to your right and take what you see."

Ali looked to the right and found a wrapped package. Inside the package, he found a shirt. When he was putting on the shirt, a piece of paper fell from the shirt pocket with the following message written on it:

> In the name of Allah, Most Gracious, Most Merciful. This is a present from the Wise, Noble Allah to Ali bin Abi Taleb. This is Harun bin Imran's shirt, "Thus it was, and We gave these as an inheritance to another people" (44:28).[50]

Virtue #41

Mohammad bin Hasan bin Ahmad narrated from Mohammad bin Husain, from Ibrahim bin Hashem, from Mohammad bin Sinan, from Ziad bin Munzer, from Saeed bin Turayf, from Asbagh bin Nobata, from Ibn Abbas, who said:

I heard the Messenger of God say, "O people! Understand that God has made a gate to Himself for you. If you enter from it, you will be safe from Hell and the great terror."

---

[50] Ghayatol Maram P660 H119. Al-Kharaej Wa Al-Jaraeh P288 H60. Bihar Al-Anwar V39 P126 H13. Ethbat Al-Hodat V4 P551 H201. Manaqeb Ibn Shar Ahoub V2 P69. Madina Al-Maajez P16 H14. Khasaes Al-Redha P25.

Then Abu Saeed Al-Khodri stood up and said, "Guide us to this door so we recognize it."

The Prophet ﷺ replied:

It is Ali bin Abi Taleb, the Master of Successors, the Commander of the Believers, brother of the Messenger of God, and God's caliph on all people. O people! Those of you who love to hold on to the firmest handle that never breaks off, stick to Ali bin Abi Taleb's WILAYAT (unconditional, unlimited authority). His WILAYAT is my WILAYAT, and obeying him is obeying me. O people! Those of you who want to know who God's decisive argument is after me, know that it is Ali bin Abi Taleb. O people! Those of you who want to follow God and His Messenger, follow Ali bin Abi Taleb and the Imams from my family because they are the keepers of my knowledge.

Then Jabir bin Abdullah Al-Ansari asked, "How many Imams are there?"

The Prophet ﷺ replied:

O Jabir! May God have mercy on you. You have asked me about the entire Islam. Their number is the number of the months. "Verily, the number of months with Allah is twelve months in Allah's book since the day He created the heavens and the earth" (9:36). Their number is equal to the number of rivers that God created with a blast when Musa bin Imran hit the rock with his staff, which is twelve. Their number is equal to the number of the chiefs of BANI ISRAEL, as God says in the Qur'an, "We raised from among them twelve chiefs" (5:12). Therefore Jabir, the Imams are twelve. The first one is Ali bin Abi Taleb and the last one is MAHDI Al-QAEM.[51]

Virtue #42

Mohammad bin Ali bin Husain bin Musa narrated from Hasan bin Mohammad bin Saeed, from Furat bin Ibrahim, from Ahmad bin Musa, from Abu Hamed Ahmad bin Dawud, from Ali bin Yahya, from Suweid, from Yazid bin Rabeei, from Amro bin Dinar, from Tawus, from Ibn Abbas, who said:

After the Prophet ﷺ led the ASR salaat, he stood up and said, "Those of you who love me and love my family, follow me."

---

[51] Al-Yaqeen P60. Ghayatol Maram P18 H15. Al-Estensar P221. Bihar Al-Anwar V36 P263 H84

So we all followed him until we reached the house of Fatema. The Prophet knocked on the door and Ali bin Abi Taleb came out of the house. His hands were stained with clay.

The Prophet said to him, "O Abal Hasan, tell the people what you saw yesterday."

Ali said:

> Yes, O Prophet, I will ransom my mother and father for you. It was ZUHR salaat time and I wanted to do WUDHU but I had no water. So I sent Hasan and Husain to get water, but they took a long time. Then I heard a voice calling me and saying, 'O Abal Hasan look to your right.' So I looked and there was a pot hanging made of gold, filled with water that was whiter than ice, sweeter than honey, and it had the fragrance of a rose. Then I did WUDHU from that water and I drank a little from it. Then I put one drop (of this water) on my head and I felt the coolness of this drop in my heart.

Then the Prophet asked, "Do you know where this pot was from?"

Ali bin Abi Taleb replied, "Allah and His Messenger know better."

The Prophet said, "The pot was from the pots of Paradise and the water was from the river of Kawthar. That one drop (you put on your head) was from under the throne of God."

Then the Prophet hugged him (Ali) and kissed his forehead and said to him, "O my love, Jibraeel was your servant yesterday. You have a great position and status in God's eyes."[52]

Virtue #43

Sharif Abu Jaafar Mohammad bin Ahmad bin Mohammad bin Isa Al-Alawi narrated from Mohammad bin Ahmad Al-Kateb, from Hammad bin Mihran, from Abdul Adhim bin Abdullah Al-Hasani, from Mohammad bin Ali, from Mohammad bin Katheer, from Ismail bin Ziad Al-Bazzaz, from Abi Idris, from Rafe', slave of Ayesha, who said:

I was a young boy serving Ayesha and when the Prophet was with her, I used to serve them.

---

[52] Ghayatol Maram P638 H4. Madinatol Maajez P96 H245.

One day, while the Prophet﷽ was sitting with Ayesha, someone knocked at the door. I opened the door and it was a maid with a covered dish, so I went back and I told Ayesha. Ayesha told me to bring her in. She came in and put the dish in front of Ayesha, and Ayesha put it in front of the Prophet﷽. So the Prophet﷽ started eating from the dish and the maid left.

Then the Prophet﷽ said, "I wish the Commander of the Believers, the Master of Muslims, and the Imam of the pious was here eating with me."

Ayesha said, "To whom are you referring that has all of these titles?"

The Prophet﷽ did not answer. Then he repeated what he said.

She (Ayesha) asked again, "To whom are you referring that has all of these titles?" But the Prophet﷽ did not answer.

Then someone knocked at the door and I opened it. It was Ali bin Abi Taleb﷽. I went back and told the Prophet﷽, and he said to bring him in.

The Prophet﷽ said, "O Abal Hasan, welcome. I wished for you twice. When you did not come, I asked God to bring you for me. So sit down and eat with me."

Then Ali﷽ sat down and ate with the Prophet﷽.

Then the Prophet﷽ said, "O Ali, may God fight those who fight you, and may God be the enemy of your enemies."

So Ayesha said, "Who will fight him and be his enemy?"

The Prophet﷽ replied to her, "You and those with you; you will accept fighting him and will not refuse it." The Prophet﷽ repeated this twice.[53]

Virtue #44

Hasan bin Hamza narrated from Ali bin Mohammad bin Qutaibah, from Fadl bin Shazan, from Mohammad bin Ziad, from Jameel bin Salih, from Jaafar bin Mohammad﷽ (6th Imam), from his father (5th Imam﷽), from his father (4th Imam﷽), from Husain bin Ali﷽, who said:

---

[53] Al-Yaqeen P61. Ghayatol Maram P16 H18. Kashf Al-ghomma V1 P343 . Tabari in Besharatol Mustafa P165. Bihar Al-Anwar V38 P351 H3. Misbah Al-Anwar P156.

The Messenger of God said:

Fatema is the blood inside my heart; her sons are the fruits of my heart;
her husband is my eyesight; the Imams from her sons are my Lord's
secretaries; and they are His extended rope between Him and His creatures.
Those who hold onto this rope will survive and those who do not will fall.[54]

Virtue #45

Abu Abdullah Mohammad bin Wahban Al-Sali narrated from Ahmad bin
Aman Al-Amery, from Abdullah bin Abdullah bin Ataba bin Abdullah bin
Masoud, from his father, from his grandfather, Abdullah bin Masoud, who
said:

I heard the Messenger of God say, "The sun has two sides: one side
gives light to the inhabitants of the heavens, and one side gives light to the
inhabitants of earth. There is writing on both sides. Do you know what is
written (on both sides of the sun)?"

We replied, "God and His Messenger know better."

The Prophet said, "The writing on the side that gives light to the
heavens says, 'Allah is the light of the heavens and earth' (24:35). The
writing on the side that gives light to the inhabitants of earth says, 'Ali is the
light of the earths.'"[55]

Virtue #46

Ahmad bin Mohammad bin Ayyoub Al-Hafez narrated from Ahmad bin Ziad,
from Ali bin Ibrahim, from his father, from Ryan bin Salt, who said:

I heard Ali bin Musa Al-Redha say:
I heard Musa bin Jaafar say:
I heard Jaafar bin Mohammad say:
I heard Mohammad bin Ali say:
I heard Ali bin Husain say:
I heard Husain bin Ali say:

---

[54] Ghayatol Maram P46 H57. Kharazmi in Maqtal Al-Husain V1 P59. Manaqeb Al-Zamakhshari P213.
Faraed Al-Semthain V2 P66 H390. Yanbee Al-Mawaddah P82. Al-Taraef P117 H180. Sirath Al-
Mostaqeem V2 P42. Bihar Al-Anwar V3 P100 H16. Al-Fathael P146. Dorar bahr Al-Manaqeb P106.
Al-Arbaeen P14. Ehqaq Al-Haq V13 P79.
[55] Bihar Al-Anwar V27 P9 H21. Madinatol Maajez P158 H432.

I heard Ali, the Commander of the Believers, say:
I heard the Messenger of God say:
I heard Jibraeel say:
I heard God say:

Ali bin Abi Taleb is My decisive argument on My creatures. He is My light in
My land and he is the trustworthy caretaker of My knowledge. I will not
allow those who know him to enter Hell, even if they disobey Me. And I will
not allow those who deny him to enter Paradise, even if they obey Me.[56]

Virtue #47

Abu Mohammad Ibrahim bin Mohammad Al-Mathari Al-Khayyadh narrated
from Mohammad bin Jaafar, from Ayyoub bin Nuh, from Ibn Mahboub, from
Ali bin Al-Rayan, from Mallak bin Atiyya, from Jaafar bin Mohammad, from
his father, from Ali bin Husain, from his father, who said:

The Messenger of God said to Ali bin Abi Taleb:

O Abal Hasan, if the beliefs of the entire creation and their good deeds were
put on one side of a scale and your good deeds, for only one day, on the
other side of the scale, your good deeds for a single day would undoubtedly
be greater than all of the good deeds of the entire creation.

In the Battle of Uhud, Allah boasted about you to his high-ranked angels. He
removed the covers from the seven heavens on that day, and Paradise and
everything in it started shining for you. The Lord of the Worlds was pleased
with what you did, and God will reward you for that day with a reward which
will make all of the prophets, the messengers, the truthful ones, and the
martyrs envy you.[57]

Virtue #48

Ahmad bin Mohammad bin Suleiman narrated from Jaafar bin Mohammad,
from Yacoub bin Yazid, from Safwan bin Yahya, from Dawud bin Al-Hasin,
from Amr bin Azinat, from Jaafar bin Mohammad (6th Imam), from his father
(5th Imam), from Ali bin Husain (4th Imam), from his father (3rd Imam),
who said :

The Messenger of God said:

---

[56] Bihar Al-Anwar V27 P116 H91. Ghayatol Maram P512 H19.
[57] Ghayatol Maram P508 H8. Yanbee Al-Mawaddah P64 and 127.

O Ali, your example in my nation is like Al-Messiah ISA [Mary's son]. His people were divided in three groups: one group were the believers and they were the Disciples; another group was against him and those were the Jews; and the third group exaggerated about his status (thought he was the son of God) so they are out of the circle of belief.

Likewise, my nation will be divided in three groups: one group is your Shia and they are the believers; one group is your enemies and they are the ones with doubt; and one group will be those who exaggerate your status (they call you God) and they are disbelievers.

Therefore, you, O Ali, your Shia, and those who love your Shia are in Paradise. Your enemies and those who exaggerate (who call you God) are in Hell.[58]

Virtue #49

Harun bin Musa narrated from Jaafar bin Ali Al-Daqaaq, from Hareth bin Mohammad, from Saeed bin Katheer, from Mohammad bin Hasan, known as Shalqan, from Jaafar bin Mohammad (6th Imam), from his father (5th Imam)⁣, from Jabir bin Abdullah Al-Ansari, who said:

I heard the Messenger of God say, "The first one who enters Paradise from among the prophets and the truthful ones is Ali bin Abi Taleb."

Then Abu Dojana stood up and asked, "Did you not tell us that God told you that Paradise is forbidden for all the prophets before you enter it, and it is forbidden for all nations before your nation enters it?"

The Prophet replied, "Yes, but do you not know that the one who carries the flag is in front of everyone and Ali will be the flag bearer on the Day of Judgement who will be in front of me. He is the owner of my flag so he will enter Paradise before I do; he will lead with the flag and I will follow directly behind him.

Then Ali stood up, his face beaming with joy, and said, "Praise the Lord that honoured us through you, O Messenger of Allah."[59]

---

[58] Bihar Al-Anwar V25. P264 H4. Kharazmi in Manaqeb P226. Misbah Al-Anwar P23. Yanbee Al-Mawaddah P109.
[59] Kharazmi in Manaqeb P227. Al-Mohtazar P97. Misbah Al-Anwar P111. Ghayatol Maram P679 H9. Tafsir Forat Al-Koufi P175. Bihar Al-Anwar V7 P209 H100. Al-Fazael P31. Al-Ekhtesas by Mufid P354. Kashf Al-Ghomma V1 P321.

Virtue #50

Abu Mohammad Harun bin Musa Al-Talakbri narrated from Abdulaziz bin
Abdullah, from Jaafar bin Mohammad, from Abdul Karim, from Qimaz Al-
A'ttar abu Qamar, from Ahmad bin Mohammad bin Al-Walid, from Rabih Ibn
Al-Jarah, from Aamash, from Abi Wael, from Abdullah bin Masoud, who said:

The Messenger of God said:

When Allah created Adam and blew from his soul to Adam's body, Adam
sneezed and said, "Alhamdulillah."

So God sent a revelation to him and said, "You praised Me, My slave. I
swear by My Glory and Magnificence that if it was not for two slaves I would
not have created you."

Adam asked, "My Lord, are they from me?

God replied, "Yes. O Adam, raise your head and look up."

Adam raised his head and saw [the following] written on the throne of God:

> There is no god except Allah: Mohammad is the Messenger of
> Allah, he is the Prophet of Mercy and Ali is the decisive argument
> of Allah. Those who know Ali's HAQQ (right) are clean and pure
> (from all that is corrupt), and those who deny his HAQQ are cursed
> and will be the failures.
>
> I swear by My honour that I take those who obey him to Paradise,
> even if they disobey Me; and I swear by My honour that I take
> those who disobey him to Hell, even if they obey Me."[60]

Virtue #51

Abu Abdullah Husain bin Ahmad bin Mohammad bin Al-Ahwal narrated in
Mohammadiyah, from Husain bin Jaafar, from Mohammad bin Yacoub, from
Mohamed bin Isa, from Nasr bin Hammad, from Shoaba bin Al-Hajjaj, from
Ayyoub Al-Sekhtiani, from Nafi', from Omar's son, who said:

The Messenger of God said:

---

[60] Kharazmi in Manaqeb P227. Ghayatol Maram P7 H16. Yanbee Al-Mawaddah P11. Misbah Al-
Anwar P94. Tabari in Besharatol Mustafa P68. Bihar Al-Anwar V68 p130 H61. Taawil Al-Ayat P47
H22. Al-Fathael P152 H79. Ehqaq Al-Haq V4 P144. Arbaeen P27. Dorar Bahr Al-Manaqeb p120.
Arjah Al-Mataleb P29.

Those of you who want to rely on Allah should love my family. Those who want to be saved from Hell should love my family. Those who want wisdom should love my family. And those who want to enter Paradise without judgement should love my family.

I swear no one loves them without succeeding in this world and in the hereafter.[61]

Virtue #52

Mohammad bin Emad Al-Tastari narrated from Mohammad bin Ahmad bin Idris, from Mohammad bin Abdullah Al-Asbahani, from his father, from Hashim, from Younis bin Ubaid, from Hasan Al-Basri, from Abdullah, who said:

The Messenger of God صلى الله عليه وآله said:

On the Day of Judgement Ali bin Abi Taleb will sit on FERDOUS, a mountain which has risen higher than Paradise. The throne of God is on top of this mountain. The rivers of Paradise blast from the sides of this mountain and flow into the gardens of Paradise.

Ali will be sitting on a chair made of light and the river of Tasneem will run in front of him. No one will be allowed to cross the bridge without a pass that states Ali's WILAYAT and the WILAYAT of his family. He oversees Paradise so only his lovers will enter it, and he oversees Hell, so only his enemies will enter it.[62]

Virtue #53

Abu Mohammad Harun bin Musa narrated from Mohammad bin Husain Al-Khathami, from Ali bin Kaab Imla, from Husain bin Thabet Al-Jammal, from his father, from Aamash, from Shafiq bin Moselma, from Hudhaifah bin Al-Yaman, who said:

The Prophet صلى الله عليه وآله stood and kissed Ali bin Abi Taleb's عليه السلام forehead and said, "O Abal Hasan you are an organ from my organs; you go where I go; and you

---

[61] Bihar Al-Anwar V27 P116 H92. Ghayatol Maram P586 H83. Kharazmi in Maqtal Al-Husain V1 P59. Faraed Al-Semthain V2 P294 H551. Al-E'teqad P296. Yanbee Al-Mawaddah P263.
[62] Bihar Al-Anwar V27 P116 H93. Ghayatol Maram P207 H12. Kharazmi in Manaqeb P31. Kharazmi in Maqtal Al-Husain V1 P39. Kashf Al-ghomma V1 P103. Ershad Al-Qolub P235 Rajeh Al-Mataleb P550. Faraed Al-Semthain V1 P292 H230. Al-manaqeb Al-Mortazawiyya P105. Yanbee Al-Mawaddah P86. Misbah Al-ANwar P60. Manaqeb Ibn Shar Ahoub V2 P7. Bihar Al-Anwar V39 P202.

have the status of intercession in Paradise. Bliss and happiness for you and
your Shia!"[63]

Virtue #54

Sahl bin Ahmad Al-Dibagi narrated from Mohammad bin Mohammad bin
Asha'th in Egypt, from Musa bin Ismail, from Abi Ismail bin Musa, from his
father, Musa bin Jaafar (7th Imam), from his father, Jaafar bin Mohammad
(6th Imam), from his father, Mohammad bin Ali (5th Imam), from his father,
Ali bin Husain (4th Imam), from his father, Husain bin Ali (3rd Imam)⁣,
who said:

The Messenger of God said, "I entered Paradise and I saw (the
following) written on its door with light:

LA ILAHA ILLALLHA
MOHAMMADUN RASOOLULLAH
ALIYUN WALIYULLAH
FATEMATU AMATULLAH (Chosen slave of Allah)
Al-HASAN WA Al-HUSAIN SEFWATULLAH (are the chosen ones)
GOD'S MERCY IS ON THOSE WHO LOVE THEM.
GOD'S CURSE IS ON THOSE WHO HATE THEM.[64]

Virtue #55

Mohammad bin Abdullah bin Abdullah Al-Hafez narrated from Jaafar bin Ali
Al-Daqaaq, from Abdullah bin Mohammad Al-Kateb, from Suleiman bin Al-
Rabia, from Nasr bin Mizahim, from Ali bin Abdullah, from Asha'th, from
Zamra, from Abi Dhar, who said:

The Prophet looked at Ali bin Abi Taleb and said:

He is the best from the first to the last of all of the inhabitants of the
heavens and the earths. He is the master of the truthful ones. He is the
beauty of the successors. He is the Imam of the pious and he is the leader of
the believers.

---

[63] Ghayatol Maram P586 H84.
[64] Ghayatol Maram P586 H82. Madinatol Maajez P149 H415. Kanz Al-Ommal P63. Bihar Al-
AnwarV27 P228 H31. Rowzat Al-Jannat V6 P181. AL-Khisal of Sadough V1 P323 H10. Amali of Tousi
V1 P365 H77. Kharazmi in Manaqeb 214. Faraed Al-Semthain V2 P73 H396. Lesan Al-Mizan V5 P70,
Kefayat Al-Taleb P423. Al-Sirath Al-Mostaghim V2 P75 H4. Kashf Al-Ghommah V1 P94. AL-Taraaef
P64 H65. Mizan Al-Eetedal V2 P217. Miftah Al-Najat P15. Dorar Bahr Al-Manaqeb P31. Kharazmi in
Maqtal Al-Husain V1 P18.

On the Day of Judgement, Ali will ride on a camel from the camels of Paradise, and the light of the camel will light the entire plain on which the judgement process will take place.

Because he will be wearing a crown made of sapphires and gems, the angels will say that Ali is a high-ranked angel and the prophets will say that he is a prophet.

Then the caller will call from inside the throne, "This is the most truthful; this is the heir of Allah's love (the Prophet ﷺ); this is Ali bin Abi Taleb."

Ali will stand on top of Hell. Whoever he does not love will enter Hell, and whoever he loves will be saved.

Then Ali will come to the gates of Paradise and his friends and Shia will enter from any door they choose, without judgement.[65]

Virtue #56

Abul Hasan Mohammad bin Jaafar Al-Nahwy narrated from his father, from Mohammad bin Hasan bin Ali Al-Qazwiny, from Ahmad bin Dawud, from Mohammad bin Saleh, from Abbas bin Rabi', from Esma bin Ismail, from Abu Ma'shar, from Abu Huraira, who said:

The Messenger of God ﷺ said:

On the night of Meraj, I heard a call from under the throne that said, "Ali is the sign of guidance and he is the heir of My love (the Prophet ﷺ) so announce it."

When I came down from the heavens, God reminded me of this incident through the revelation of this verse, "O Messenger, deliver what has been sent down to you from your Lord. And if you do not do it (it will be as if) you have not delivered His message (at all)" (5:67).[66]

Virtue #57

The judge, Al-Moaafi bin Zakariyya, narrated from Mohammad bin Mazid, from Abu Karib Mohammad bin Alaa, from Ismail bin Sabih, from Abu Younis, from Mohammad bin Al-Monkder, from Jabir bin Abdullah Al-Ansari, who said:

---

[65] Ghayatol Maram P46 H56. Bihar Al-Anwar V26 P316 H81.
[66] Ghayatol Maram P207 H13. Madinatol Maajez P160 H405. Misabah Al-Anwar P49. Shawahed Al-Tanzil V1 P187 h242. Faraed Al-Semthain v1 p158.

The Messenger of God ﷺ said to Ali bin Abi Taleb ؑ:

Are you not pleased that you are to me as Harun was to Musa, except that there is no prophet after me? And if there were to be one, it would have been you.[67]

Virtue #58

Abu Mohammad Hasan bin Ali bin Abdullah Al-Alwy Al-Taabari narrated from Ahmad bin Mohammad bin Abdullah, from his grandfather, from his father, from Hammad bin Isa, from Amr bin Azina, from Aban bin Abi Ayyash, from Suleim bin Qays Al-Helali, from Salman Al-Mohammadi, who said:

I went to the Prophet ﷺ and saw Husain ؑ on his lap. He (the Prophet ﷺ) was kissing Husain's ؑ forehead and lips and he said:

You are a Sayyid (Master), son of a Sayyid, and father of the Sayyids. You are an Imam, the son of an Imam, and father of the Imams. You are God's decisive argument, the son of God's decisive argument, and you are the father of nine of God's decisive arguments, and the ninth one is the QAEM.[68]

Virtue #59

Abul Qassem Ubaidullah bin Hasan bin Mohammad Al-Sokouni narrated from Hasan bin Mohammad Al-Baghli, from Ahmad bin Yahya bin Husain bin Zaid bin Ali, from his father, from his grandfather, Husain bin Zaid, who said:

Imam Jaafar bin Mohammad ؑ said, "My father told me that his father told him that his father told him that his father, the Commander of the Believers ؑ, said:

---

[67] Ghayatol Maram P119 H74. Kanz Al-Ommal P282. Boghyat Al-Woaat P452. Khatib in Tarikh Al-Baghdad V3 P288. Tarikh Demashq V1 P346 H427. Amali of Tousi V2 P211 H15. Bihar Al-Anwar V37 P255 H5. Ethbat Al-Hodat V3 P452 H464. Arbaeen P39. Faraed Al-Semthain V1 P123 H86. Zail Al-Laali P59. Lesan Al-Mizan V5 H378.Taraef P51.Arjah AL-Mataleb P431. Ehqaq Al-Haq V16 P86, Kharazmi In Maqtal Al-Husain V1 P48.
[68] Ghayatol Maram P46 H59. Kharazmi in Maqtal Al-Husain V1 P146. Helyat Al-Abrar V2 P720 H128. Al-Taraaef P174 H272. Al-Sirath Al-Mostaqeem V2 P119. Al-Emama Wa Al-Tabserah P110. Ekmal Al-Deen V1 P272 H9. Oyoun Akhbar Al-Redha V1 P52 H17. Al-Khesal P475 H38. Bihar Al-Anwar V36 P241 H47. Kefayatol Athar P45. Mawaddat Al-Qorba P95. Al-Manaqeb Al-Mortazawiyyah P129. Yanbee Al-Mawaddah P168. Arjah Al-Mataleb P448. Ehqaq Al-Haq V13 P71-71. Kashf Al-ghomma V3 P298. Al-Ensaf P164 H172.

"God's curse is on those who do not say that I am the fourth of the four caliphs."

So Husain bin Zaid said to Jaafar bin Mohammed, "But you say that he is the first caliph of the Prophet, and you do not lie."

Jaafar bin Mohammad replied:

> Yes. God says in the Qur'an, "When Your Lord said to the angels: Verily I am going to appoint a caliph in the earth" (2:30). So Adam was the first caliph. And God says in the Qur'an, "O Dawud! Verily we have appointed you as a caliph in the earth" (38:26). So Dawud was the second caliph. And God says in the Qur'an, "Musa said to Harun, take my place (be my caliph) among my people, act rightly" (7:142). So Harun was the third caliph, and Ali is the caliph of Mohammad. That is why Ali said that God's curse is on those who do not say that he is the fourth of the four caliphs.[69]

Virtue #60

Abu Hafs Amr bin Ibrahim bin Ahmad bin Katheer Al-Makri narrated from Abdullah bin Mohammad bin Abdalaziz Al-Baghawey, from Abdullah bin Omar, from Abdul Malik bin Umair, from Salem Al-Bazzaz, from Abu Huraira, who said:

The Messenger of God said, "Ali bin Abi Taleb, Fatema, Hasan, and Husain are the best of this nation after me. God's curse is on whoever says anything against this."[70]

Virtue #61

Abul Tayyeb Mohammad bin Husain Al-Teimali narrated from Ali bin Abbas, from Bakkar bin Ahmad, from Nasr bin Muzahim, from Ziad bin Al-Monzir, from Al-Monzir, from Salman [the Farsi], who said:

The Messenger of God said:

O Salman, those who love Fatema, my daughter, will be with me in Paradise, and those who hate her will be in Hell.

---

[69] Ghayatol Maram P69 H19. Al-Borhan V1 P75 H13. Madinatol Maajez P160. Manaqeb Ibn Shar Ahoub V2 P261. Bihar Al-Anwar V38 P153 H127.
[70] Ghayatol Maram P450 H16. Kanz Al-Ommal P63. Bihar Al-Anwar V27 P228 H31. Rowzat Al-Jannat V6 H181.

O Salman, the love of Fatema will be beneficial in one hundred difficult instances. The least difficult of these instances will be at the time of death, in the grave, at the scale, the gathering of people on the Day of Judgement, the bridge, the display (of your book), and the calculation.

I am pleased with those with whom Fatema is pleased, and God is pleased with those with whom I am pleased.

I am angry with those with whom Fatema is angry, and God is angry with those with whom I am angry.

Woe unto those who are unjust to her and to her husband, the Commander of the Believers.

Woe unto those who are unjust to her Shia and to her progeny.[71]

Virtue #62

Abul Hasan Ahmad bin Al-Hasan Al-Dhahhak Al-Razi narrated from Hamza bin Abdullah Al-Maleki, from Abdullah bin Mohammad Rasmoeh, from Ibn Harma, from Anas bin Malik, who said:

The Messenger of God﷽ asked me to saddle his mule, so I did. Then the Prophet﷽ rode and I followed him. When we arrived at the house of the Commander of the Believers﷽, the Prophet﷽ asked me to saddle Ali's﷽ mule, so I did. The Prophet﷽ and Ali﷽ rode together and I was following them until they came to a green and beautiful land. Then a white cloud covered them so I went closer and I heard a loud voice saying:

"ASSALAMU ALAIKUMA WA RAHMATULLAH WA BARAKATU."

They answered the salaam. Then Jibraeel came down, and then I could no longer see them. Then when Jibraeel went back up, I saw the Prophet﷽ call Ali﷽. The Prophet﷽ gave Ali﷽ an apple that had the following statement written on it, "This is a present from the Predominant Lord to his WALI, Ali bin Abi Taleb."[72]

---

[71] Bihar Al-Anwar V27 P116 H94. Ghayatol Maram P18 H17. Kharazmi in Maqtal Al-Husain V1 P59. Yanbee Al-Mawaddah P263. Mawaddat Al-Qorba P116. Ehqaq Al-Haq V10 P166.
[72] Madinatol Maajez V61 H132.

Virtue #63

Abu Abdullah Ahmad bin Mohammad bin Al-Hasan bin Ayyoub Al-Hafez narrated from Abu Ali Ahmad bin Mohammad bin Jaafar Al-Souli, from Mohammad bin Husain, from Hafs bin Omar, from Abu Mu'awiyah, from Aamash, from Abu Wael, from Abdullah, son of Omar, who said:

The Messenger of God said:

"Jibraeel told me that Ali is the best human being. Those who deny this are KAFERS."[73]

Virtue #64

Hasan bin Ahmad bin Sokhtoeh Al-Mojawer narrated from Mohammad bin Ahmad Al-Baghdadi, from Isa bin Mihran, from Yahya bin Abdul Hamid Al-Hamani, from Qays bin Rabia, from Aamash, from Abi Wael, from Abdullah bin Masoud, who said:

The Messenger of God said:

The first inhabitants of the heavens to take Ali bin Abi Taleb as a brother, were Israfil, then Mikaeel, and then Jibraeel. The first ones to love him were the carriers of the throne, then Rezwan, the keeper of Paradise, and then the angel of death.

The angel of death is as merciful to those who love Ali bin Abi Taleb as he is to the prophets.[74]

Virtue #65

Talha bin Ahmad bin Mohammad bin Zakariyya Al-Nishabori narrated from Sanah bin Abdul Rahman bin Ali bin Abdullah bin Abdul Hamid, from Hashim bin Bashir, from Shaba, bin Al-Hajjaj, from Ali bin Thabet, from Abi Saeed Al-Khodri, from Ibn Abbas, who said:

---

[73] Bihar Al-Anwar V26 P306 H66. Ghayatol Maram P450 H15. Amail of Sadough P71 H7. Oyoun Akhbar Al-Redha V2 P59 H225. Faraed Al-Semthain V1 P154 H116. Tarikh Al-Baghdad V3 P192. Tahthib Al-Tahthib V9 P419 . Kanz Al-Ommal V12 P221 H1286 . Kefayat Al-Taleb H245. Miftah Al-Najaat P49. Ethbat AL-Hodat V3 P634 H867. Amali of Sadough P71 H6. Amali of Tousi P213. Nawader Al-Athar fi Ali Khair Al-Bashar P23-42. Tarikh Baghdad V7 P421. Al-Montakhab V5 P35. Al-Fathael Ahmad bin Hanbal P46 H72. Sirath Al-Mostaqeem V2 P70. Tajhiz Al-Jaysh P308. Lesan Al-Mizan V3P166. Misbah Al-Anwar P138. Al-Riyath Al-Nazerah V2 P220.
[74] Kharazmi in Manaqeb P31. Kharazmi In Maqtal V1 P30. Manaqeb Shahr Ahoub V2 P32. Yanabee Al-Mawaddah P133. Kashf Al-Ghomma V1 P103. Ghayatol Maram P580 H26. Misbah Al-Anwar P61. Bihar Al-ANwar V38 P335 H10. Ehqaq Al-Haq V6 P111.

I heard the Messenger of God say that on the night of Meraj he entered Paradise and he saw a light that was very bright. So he asked Jibraeel about the light.

Jibraeel replied, "O Mohammad, this light is not from the sun nor is it from the moon. This (light) is from one of Ali bin Abi Taleb's maids. She came out of her palace and she looked at you and smiled. The light that you saw was from her teeth, and she will walk around in Paradise until the Commander of the Believers, Ali bin Abi Taleb, will enter Paradise."[75]

Virtue #66

Abu Abdullah Husain bin Mohammad bin Ishaq bin Abi Khattab Al-Suoti narrated from Ismail bin Ali Al-Daabeli, from his father, from Ali bin Musa Al-Redha (8th Imam), from his father(7th Imam), from Jaafar bin Mohammad (6th Imam), from his father(5th Imam), from Ali bin Husain (4th Imam), from his father (3rd Imam), who said:

The Messenger of God said to Ali bin Abi Taleb, "O Ali you are the best human being. Those who doubt this are KAFERS."[76]

Virtue #67

Al-Sharif Al-Naqib Abu Mohammad Al-Hasan bin Mohammad Al-Aalawy Al-Hussayni narrated from Mohammad bin Zakariyya, from Abbas bin Bakkar, from Abu Bakr Al-Hozali, from Akrama, from Ibn Abbas, who said:

The Messenger of God said to Abdul Rahman bin Awf:

O Abdul Rahman, you people are my companions, but Ali bin Abi Taleb is from me and I am from him. So those who compare him to anyone are unjust to me. Those who are unjust to me, hurt me. God's curse is on those who hurt me.

O Abdul Rahman, Allah sent His book to me and ordered me to teach it to all people, except Ali bin Abi Taleb, because he does not need to be taught. God made Ali's eloquence as my eloquence, and Ali's knowledge as my knowledge.

---

[75] Ghayatol Maram P18 H18. Al-Yaqeen P61. Kharazmi in Manaqeb P227. and in Maqtal P39. Kefayatol Taleb P321. Ethbat Al-Hodat V4 P64 H482. .Al-Mohtazar P99.
[76] Bihar Al-Anwar V26 P306 H67. Ghayatol Maram P450 H17.

If patience was a person, it would be Ali bin Abi Taleb; and if moral excellence was a person it would be Hasan; and if modesty was a person it would be Husain; and if everything that is good were to be a person it would be Fatema, and she is even better than that.

The origin of my daughter, Fatema, is greater than any other inhabitant on earth, as is her honour and her generosity.[77]

Virtue #68

The judge, Al-Moaafi bin Zakariyya narrated from Ibrahim bin Fadl, from Fadl bin Yousef, from Hasan bin Saber, from Wakeh, from Hisham bin Urwah, from his father, from Ayesha, who said:

The Messenger of God said, "Mentioning Ali bin Abi Taleb is worshiping God."[78]

Virtue #69

Abul Qassem Jaafar bin Masrur Al-Lahham narrated from Husain bin Mohammad, from Ibrahim bin Mohammad, from Bilal, from Ibrahim bin Saleh Al-Anmati, from Abdul Samad, from Jaafar bin Mohammad (6th Imam), from his father (5th Imam), from Ali bin Husain (4th Imam), from his father (3rd Imam), who said:

The Prophet was asked to explain this verse, "Those who believe and do good, for them is bliss (TOUBA) and a beautiful place of return" (13:29). The Prophet explained that this verse refers to the Commander of the Believers, Ali, and that TOUBA is a tree in his house in FERDOUS.[79]

Every house in Paradise has a fruitful branch from this tree.[80]

---

[77] Ghayatol Maram P512 H20. Kharazmi in Maqtal Al-Husain V1 P60. Faraed Al-Semthain V2 P68 H392.
[78] Kharazmi in Manaqeb P261. Tarikh Demeshgh V2 P424. Al-Manaqeb of Moghazeli P206 H 243. Al-Ferdous P110. Manaqeb Ibn Shar Ahoub V3 P6. kanz Al-Ommal V12 P201. Al-Montakhab V5 P30 . Yanabee Al-Mawaddah P237 H261. Bihar Al-Anwar V38 P199. Konouz Al-Haqayeq P78. Yanabee Al-Mawaddah P180. Al-Bedaya Wa Al-Nehaye V7 P357. AL-Jame Al-Sagheer V1 P583. Al-Fath AlKabeer V2 p120. Mawaddat Al-Qorba V7 P111.
[79] Note from Translator: Please refer to Virtue #52 for more details about FERDOUS.
[80] Al-Yaqeen P62. Ghayatol Maram P19 H19. Bihar Al-Anwar v39 p235 h20. Manaqeb Ibn Shar Ahoub V3 P32. Majmaa Al-Bayan V6 P291. Al-Taraef p100 h147. Al-Omdah P183 . Shawahed Al-Tanzil V1 P304 H417. Manaqb Al-Moghazeli P268 H315. Dor Al-Manthour V4 P59.

Virtue #70

Abul Qassem Abdullah bin Mohammad bin Ishaq bin Suleiman bin Hananah
Al-Bazzaz narrated from Al-Baghawey Abdullah bin Mohammad, from Hasan
bin Arafah, from Zajr bin Harun, from Jamil bin Al-Taweel, from Anas, from
Ayesha:

Ayesha said, "I heard the Messenger of Godﷺ say that Ali؏ is the best
human being. Those who deny this are KAFERS."

So people asked her, "Why did you go to war with him?"

Ayesha replied, "I did not do this out of my own inclination. It was Talha and
Zubair that made me fight him."[81]

Virtue #71

The scholar, Abu Bakr Mohammad bin Abdullah bin Hamdun bin Al-Fadl,
narrated from the judge, Abdul Rahman bin Hasan, from Ibrahim bin Husain,
from Shah Abdullah bin Salma Al-Saqir, from Shoba bin Al-Hajjaj Abu Rajaa
Al-Attar, from Samarah, who said:

Every morning the Prophetﷺ would come to his companions and ask,
"Has anyone had a dream?"

One morning the Prophetﷺ came and said:

> I saw Hamza, my uncle, and Jaafar, my cousin, in my dream. They
> were sitting and eating from a dish of figs that they had in front of
> them. The figs changed to dates, and they continued eating. So I
> asked them what they found was the best thing to do to prepare
> for the hereafter. They said Salaat, loving Ali bin Abi Taleb؏, and
> giving charity secretly.[82]

Virtue #72

The scholar, Abu Bakr Mohammad bin Abdullah bin Hamdun bin Al-Fadl,
narrated from the judge, Abdul Rahman bin Hasan, from the scholar, Abul
Faraj Mohammad bin Al-Mozaffar bin Qays Al-Makri's narration, from Hasan
bin Mohammad bin Saeed, from Saraba bin Ibrahim, from Ali bin

---

[81] Bihar Al-Anwar V26 P306 H68. Al-Mohtazar p551.
[82] Bihar Al-Anwar V27 P117 H95. Madinat Al-Majez P172 H476.

Mohammad bin Mokhled, from Jaafar bin Hifz, from Mohammad bin Ismail, from Zaid bin Eiad, from Safwan bin Salman, from Salman bin Yassar, from Ibn Abbas, who said:

The Messenger of God ﷺ said:

Ali bin Abi Taleb is like my skin to me; he is like my flesh; he is like my bones; and he is like the blood that flows in my veins. Ali is my brother, my heir, my caliph; he repays my debts[83]; and he fulfills my commitments. Ali is my replacement in the world when I die.[84]

Virtue #73

Abul Faraj Mohammad bin Muzaffar bin Ahmad bin Saeed Al-Daqaaq narrated from Ahmad bin Mohammad, from Mohammad bin Mansour, from Uthman bin Abi Shiba, from Jurrair, from Mohammad bin Yassar, from Fadl bin Harun, from Abi Harun Al-Abdi, from Abi Bakr Abdullah bin Uthman, who said:

We were with the Prophet ﷺ in Amer bin Saad's garden. As we were walking in the garden, we heard a palm tree shout to another palm tree.

Then the Prophet ﷺ asked, "Do you know what the palm tree said?"

We replied, "God and His Messenger know better."

The Prophet ﷺ said, "The palm tree shouted 'This is Mohammad, the Messenger of God ﷺ , and his heir, Ali bin Abi Taleb ﷺ."

So the Prophet ﷺ named the palm tree "Al-Nakhlah Al-Sayhani" (the shouting palm tree).[85]

---

[83] Note from Translator: People would store their valuable things with the Prophet ﷺ.
[84] Ghayatol Maram P69 H20.
[85] Madinatol Maajez P65 H152. Thaqeb Al-Manaqeb P34 H17. Kharazmi in Manaqeb P221. Sirath Al-Mostaqeem V2 P33. Ethbat AL-Hodat V5 P64 H439. Faraed AL-Semthain V1 P137. Yanabee Al-Mawadda P136. Ghayatol Maram P157 H26. AL-Kharaej Wa Al-Jaraeh P478. Bihar AL-Anwar V17 P365 H7. Manqeb Ibn shahr Ashoub V2 P153. Al-Fathael of Shathan bin Jibraeel P146 H113. Mizan Al-Eetedal (Zahabi) P79. Lesan Al-Mizan V1 P317. Sirat Al-Zahabiyya V2 P256. Dorar Bahr Al-Manaqeb P105. Kholasatol Wafaa P39. Meftah Al-Najat. Arbaeen. Arjah Al-Mataleb P36. Nazm Dorar Al-Semthain P124. Ehqaq Al-Haq V4 P112.

Virtue #74

Hasan bin Ali Al-Wafawy from Al-Abbas bin Bakkar Al-Dhaabi, from Abu Bakr Al-Hozali, from Akrama, from Ibn Abbas, who said:

Someone asked Ibn Abbas to describe the family of the Prophetﷺ. Ibn Abbas replied:

> They are the pious teachers.
> They are extremely generous.
> They ignore their own desires.
> They are destroyers of every evil.
> They are disinterested in the world.
> They do not have any worldly ambitions.
> They are the polite ones.
> They are aware at all times.
> They are professional horsemen.[86]
> They are the stars at night.
> They are the Nile sea.[87]
> They are oblivious to human desire.
> They are the highest (in status) of all heights.
> They are the masters of the masters.
> They are the rain of mercy on those who need them.
> They are the brave lions.
> They are the establishers of Salaat.
> They are the givers of Zakat.
> They perform the good deeds.
> They are the destroyers of bad deeds.[88]

Virtue #75

Mohammad bin Ali bin Fadl Al-Zaiaat from Husain bin Mohammad, from Hasan bin Rabi' Al-Magshoni, from Ismail bin Aban Al-Warraq, from Ghiyath bin Ibrahim, from Jaafar bin Mohammad (6th Imam), from his father (5th Imam), from Ali bin Husain (4th Imam), from his father (3rd Imam)ﷺ, who said:

The Messenger of Godﷺ said:

Jibraeel came to him one morning, very happy and optimistic.

---

[86] Note from Translator: This was one of the most important traits for any leader.
[87] Note from translator: " Sea" is the most common way of expressing generosity in the Arabic language and the Nile was known to be one of the largest seas.
[88] Lesan Al-Mizan V3 P237 H1052.

So the Prophet asked, "Why you are so happy?"

Jibraeel replied, "How can I not be happy after seeing how God honoured you and your brother, the Imam of your nation, Ali bin Abi Taleb?"

The Prophet asked, "How did God honour the Imam of my nation (Ali bin Abi Taleb) and I?"

Jibraeel replied:

> Last night God boasted about Ali worshiping Him to His angels and to those who carry His throne. He told them, 'Look at My decisive argument (Ali bin Abi Taleb) in My land after My Prophet. Look at how he kneels with his forehead on the ground for Me out of humility. I take you (angels and the carriers of the throne) as witnesses that he is the Imam and the master of My creation.[89]

Virtue #76

Abu Bakr Mohammad bin Abdullah bin Hamdun narrated from Mohammad bin Ahmad, from Jaafar bin Mohammad bin Shaker Al-Saegh, from Mansour bin Sifr, from Mahdi bin Maimun, from Mohammad bin Sereen, from his brother, Maabad, from Abi Saeed Al-Khodri, who said:

The Messenger of God asked God, "O Allah, appoint one minister for me from among the inhabitants of the heavens and another one from among the inhabitants of earth."

So God sent him a revelation and said, "I appoint Jibraeel as your minister from among the inhabitants of the heavens, and I appoint Ali bin Abi Taleb as your minister from among the inhabitants of earth."[90]

Virtue #77

Jaafar bin Mohammad (6th Imam) narrated from his father (5th Imam), from Ali bin Husain (4th Imam), from his father (3rd Imam), from the Commander of the Believers, from The Messenger of God, from Jibraeel, from God, who said:

---

[89] Borhan V1 P27 H14. Kharazmi in Manaqeb P236. Kharazmi in Maqtal Al-Husain V1 P47.Ghayatol Maram P214 H24. Yanbee Al-Mawaddah P629 H7.
[90] Ghayatol Maram P613 H9.

Those who testify, "There is no God but Me; Mohammad is My slave and My Messenger; Ali bin Abi Taleb is My caliph; and his sons are My decisive arguments," I will allow them to enter My Paradise with My mercy. I will save them from Hell with My forgiveness. They will be My neighbours, and I will honour them. I will give them My complete grace and I will make them among the special and chosen ones.

If they call Me, I will respond. If they pray to Me, I will answer them. If they ask Me (anything), I will grant it to them. If they do not initiate (coming to Me), I will initiate (it). If they commit mistakes, I will have mercy on them.

If they run from Me, I will invite them to Myself. If they come back to Me, I will accept them. If they knock on My door, I will open it."

And those who do not testify that, "There is no God except Me, or do testify that, but do not testify that Mohammad is My slave and My messenger, or do testify that, but do not testify that Ali bin Abi Taleb is My caliph, or do testify that, but do not testify that the Imams from his sons are My decisive arguments, they (those who do not testify completely) do not believe in My blessings. They disrespect Me; they are KAFERS; and they do not believe in My signs, My books, and My messengers.

If they come to Me, I will hide Myself from them. If they ask Me (anything), I will not grant it. If they call Me, I will not hear their call. If they pray to Me, I will ignore them. If they want Me, I will disappoint them. And this is their punishment from Me, and I am not unjust to My slaves."[91]

Virtue #78

Abu Bakr Mohammad bin Abdullah bin Hamdun narrated from Mohammad bin Ahmad, from Jaafar bin Mohammad bin Shaker, the jeweler, from Mansour bin Sifr, from Mahdi bin Maimun, from Mohammad bin Sereen, from his brother, Maabad, from Abi Saeed Al-Khodri, who said:

The Messenger of God ﷺ said:

Knowledge is divided in five parts. Four of those parts are given to Ali bin Abi Taleb and the last part is shared among all people. I swear to God, who sent me as a Prophet, that Ali bin Abi Taleb is more knowledgeable than all people, even in relation to the one part (of knowledge) that is given to them.[92]

---

[91] Meato manghaba footnote of H92. (H77 of the original book is a copy of H75. That is why we have selected this HADITH from the footNote of H92.)
[92] Ghayatol Maram P512 H21 and P586 H85. Bihar Al-Anwar V27 P117H96.

Virtue #79

Abu Mohammad bin Farid Al-Boshangi narrated from Zubair bin Bakkar, from Sufyan bin Eiina, from Abu Qalaba, from Ayyoub Al-Sekhtiani, from Anas bin Malik, who said:

I was standing in front of the Prophet صلى الله عليه وآله in his mosque in Medina. He told me to go and bring Ali bin Abi Taleb عليه السلام quickly for him.

I went and found Ali عليه السلام (Fatema عليها السلام was with him), and I told him that the Prophet صلى الله عليه وآله wanted to see him. He came with me immediately.

When we got to the Prophet صلى الله عليه وآله, Ali عليه السلام said salaam to the Prophet صلى الله عليه وآله.

The Prophet صلى الله عليه وآله said, "O Ali, say salaam to Jibraeel."

So Ali عليه السلام said, "Assalamo Alaik O Jibraeel." Jibraeel answered his salaam.

The Prophet صلى الله عليه وآله told Ali عليه السلام that Jibraeel said:

> God sends His salaam to you (Ali عليه السلام) and says, 'Bliss and happiness for you and your Shia and those who love you. And woe and more woe on those who hate you. On the Day of Judgement, the caller will call from inside the throne and will say, 'Where are Mohammad and Ali?' Then you both will go up to the seventh sky and will stand in front of God.
>
> Then God will say to His Prophet, 'Take Ali to the Pool of Kawthar and give him this cup so he can distribute the water to his lovers and his Shia, but not to those who hate him.'
>
> Then God will say, 'He (Ali عليه السلام) will order that his lovers have an easy judgement process and he will order that they enter Paradise.'[93]

Virtue #80

Ahmad bin Mohammad bin Saeed narrated from Husain bin Mahfuz, from Ahmad bin Ishaq, from Ghatrifi bin Abdul Salam, from Abdul Razzaq, from Mo'ammar, from Zohari Abu Bakr Abdullah bin Abdul Rahman, from Uthman

---

bin A'ffan, from Omar bin Al-Khattab, from Abu Bakr bin Abi Quhaafa, who said:

I heard the Messenger of God 🖐 say that: ·

God has created angels from the light of Ali bin Abi Taleb's face. All they do is praise and sanctify the Lord, the THAWAB (reward) of which they dedicate to those who love Ali and to those who love his sons.[94]

Virtue #81

The Chief of Justice, Abu Abdullah Al-Husain bin Harun Al-Daabi narrated from Ahmad bin Mohammad, from Ali bin Hasan, from his father, from Ali bin Musa Al-Redha (8th Imam), from his father (7th Imam), from Jaafar bin Mohammad (6th Imam), from his father (5th Imam), from Ali bin Al-Husain (4th Imam), from his father, (Imam Husain)🖐, who said:

The Messenger of God 🖐 said, "There will be a dark conspiracy after me. The only survivors will be 'those who hold on to the firmest handle' (2:256)."

So the people asked the Prophet 🖐, "What is the firmest handle?"

The Prophet 🖐 replied, "The WILAYAT of the Master of the Successors."

They asked the Prophet 🖐, "Who is the Master of the Successors?"

The Prophet 🖐 replied, "The Commander of the Believers."

They asked the Prophet 🖐, "Who is the Commander of the Believers?"

The Prophet 🖐 replied, "The Master of Muslims and their Imams after me."

They asked the Prophet 🖐, "Who is the Master of Muslims and their Imams after you?"

The Prophet 🖐 replied, "My brother, Ali bin Abi Taleb."[95]

---

[94] Ghayatol Maram p8 h19. Bihar Al-Anwar V27 P118 H98. madinat Al-Maajez P188 H515. Kharazmi in Maqtal of Husain V1 P97. Misbah Al-Anwar P297. Jame Al-Akhbar P212
[95] Bihar Al-Anwar V36 P20 H16. BorhanV1 P244 H11. Al-Yaqeen P62. Ghayatol Maram P19 H2o and P46 H61 and P167 H62.

Virtue #82

Husain bin Mohammad bin Mihran Al-Damghani narrated from Mohammad
Ibn Abdullah bin Nasr, from Abdullah bin Al-Mobark Al-Dainouri, from Hasan
bin Ali, from Mohammad bin Abdullah bin Urwah, from Yousef bin Bilal, from
Mohammad bin Marwan, from Al-Saeb, from Abi Saleh, from Ibn Abbas, who
said:

The Messenger of God ﷺ said:

I was going up with Jibraeel on the night of Meraj. When we reached the
fourth sky, I saw a house made of rubies.

Jibraeel said to me "O Mohammad, this is BAIT Al-MA'MOUR' (Qiblah of the
inhabitants of the skies). God created this house fifty thousand years before
He created the heavens and the earths. O Mohammad, pray towards this
house."

Then God ordered all of the other prophets and messengers to come.
Jibraeel aligned them (all of the other prophets and messengers) in one line
behind me and I led the SALAAT (prayers).

When I finished the SALAAT, God sent someone to me who said, "O
Mohammad, God sends his Salaam to you. God wants you to ask the
messengers what their message was to the people before you."

So I asked the messengers, "With what message did God send you?"

They replied, "The message was your WILAYAT and the WILAYAT of Ali bin
Abi Taleb."

Then the Prophet referred to this verse, "Ask those of our messengers whom
we sent before you" (43:45).[96]

Virtue #83

Abu Mohammad Abdullah bin Husain Sheikh Al-Saleh narrated from
Mohammad bin Ali Al-Aaraj, from Mohammad bin Al-Husain bin Abdul
Wahhab, from Ali bin Husain, from Rabia bin Yazid Al-Raqashi, from Anas bin
Malik, who said:

The Messenger of God ﷺ said:

---

[96] Ghayatol Maram P207 H14. Bihar Al-Anwar V26 P307 H69.

54

Ali bin Abi Taleb will be called with seven names on the Day of Judgement:

> O SEDDIQ (The Truthful)
> O DAAL (The Guide)
> O A'BED (The Worshipper)
> O HADI (The Guide)
> O MAHDI (The one on the right way)
> O FATA (The Fearless Man)
> O ALI (The High)

You (Ali) and your Shia will enter Paradise without judgement.[97]

Virtue #84

Mohammad bin Abdullah bin Abdul Muttaleb bin Matar Al-Shaibani narrated from Abdullah bin Saeed, from Moammal bin Ahab, from Abdul Razzaq Mo'ammar, from Al-Zohari, from Urwah, from Ayesha, who said:

Ali bin Abi Taleb﷽ came to my father (Abu Bakr) while he was ill with the illness that caused his death. My father was staring at his (Ali's﷽) face and would not take his eyes off of him.

So when Ali bin Abi Taleb﷽ left, I asked my father, "Why were you looking at his face like that?"

He (Abu Bakr) replied, "Because I heard the Messenger of God﷽ say, 'Looking at Ali's face is worshiping God.'"[98]

Virtue #85

Jaafar bin Mohammad bin Qoloeh narrated from Ali bin Hasan Al-Nahwy, from Ahmad bin Mohammad, from Mansour bin Abi Abbas, from Ali bin Asbat, from Hakam bin Bohloul, from Abu Humam Abdullah bin Adhina, from Jaafar bin Mohammad (6th Imam), from his father (5th Imam), from Ali bin Al-Husain (4th Imam), from his father (Imam Husain)﷽, who said:

---

[97] Kharazmi in Manaqeb P228.Ghayatol Maram P587 H88. Ehqaq Al-Haq V4 P299. Misbah Al-Anwar P95.
[98] Bihar Al-Anwar V26 P229 H11. Ghayatol Maram P327 H21. Amali al-sadough P119 H9. Kashf al-ghommah V1 P112. Taawil al-ayat P283. Helyatol abrar V1 P290. amali al-tousi V1 P70. Tarikh Demashq V2 P403.

Omar bin Al-Khattab stood up and said to the Prophet☀️, "You keep telling Ali bin Abi Taleb☀️, 'You are to me like Harun was to Musa', but God mentioned Harun's name in the Qur'an but did not mention Ali☀️."

The Prophet☀️ replied to him, "O disgusting Bedouin! Have you not heard this verse, 'This is the straight path that leads to me.' (15:41)?"[99] [100]

Virtue #86

Mohammad bin Ali bin Sokkar narrated from Mohammad bin Qassem, from Abbad bin Yacoub, from Shareek, from Rakeen bin Rabi', from Qassem bin Ehasan, from Zaid bin Thabet, who said:

The Messenger of God☀️ said, "I leave behind two important weights: the Qur'an and Ali bin Abi Taleb. Understand that Ali bin Abi Taleb is better than the Qur'an because he is the interpreter of the Qur'an for you."[101]

Virtue #87

The judge, Abul Faraj Al-Moaafi bin Zakariyya, narrated from Mohammad bin Ali bin Abdul Hamid bin Ziar bin Yahya Al-Quraishi, from Abdul Razzaq, from Sadagha Al-A'basi, from Zathan, from Salman Al-Mohammadi, who said:

I went to the Prophet☀️ and said salaam to him. Then I went to Fatema's☀️ house and I said salaam to her.

She replied, "O Aba Abdullah (Salman), Hasan and Husain☀️ are hungry, and they are crying. Take their hands and take them to their grandfather."

So I carried them to the Prophet☀️. The Prophet☀️ asked, "O my two loves, what is wrong?"

Hasan and Husain☀️ replied, "We are hungry, O Messenger of Allah."

Then the Prophet☀️ said three times, "O Allah, feed them."

Then I saw a quince in the Prophet's☀️ hands that looked whiter than milk, sweeter than honey, and softer than butter. The Prophet☀️ rubbed it

---

[99] Note from Translator: Some translations translate this verse as, "The path of Ali is a straight path."
[100] Ghayatol Maram P119 H75. Bihar Al-Anwar V35 P58 H12. Manaqeb Ibn Shahr Ahoub V2 P302.
[101] Ghayatol Maram P214 H20. Al-Borhan V1 P28 H15. Ershad Al-Gholoub P387.

with his thumb and cut it into two pieces. He gave half to Hasan🕮 and the other half to Husain🕮. So I was looking at the two halves in their hands and I desired it.

The Prophet🕮 asked me, "O Salman, do you want some?"

I replied, "Yes, O Messenger of Allah."

The Prophet🕮 said "O Salman, this food is from Paradise. No one can eat it before completing the judgement process and being saved from Hell, even though you are on the right path."[102]

Virtue #88

Abu Sahl Mahmoud bin Omar bin Mahmoud Al-Askari narrated from Mohammad bin Omar, from Yousef bin Yacoub, from Muslim bin Ibrahim, from Hisham Al-Dostoaey, from Yahya bin Abi Katheer, from Abi Salma, from Abu Huraira, who said:

The Messenger of God🕮 said:

God has created one hundred thousand angels in the fourth sky and three hundred angels in the fifth sky. God has created one angel in the seventh sky that is so big that his head is under the throne of God and his feet touch the earth, and Allah has created many more angels.

The only sustenance for these angels is SALAWAT on Ali, the Commander of the Believers, and on his lovers, and seeking forgiveness for the sins of his Shia and for his lovers.[103]

Virtue #89

Ahmad bin Mohammad bin Musa bin Urwah narrated from Mohammad bin Uthman Al-Moa'ddel, from Mohammad bin Abdul Malik, from Yazid bin Harun, from Hammad bin Salma, from Thabet, from Anas bin Malik, who said:

I saw the Prophet🕮 in my dream and he asked me:

---

[102] Madinatol Maajez P216 H60. Bihar Al-Anwar V43 P308 H72. Al-Awalem V16 P62 H2. Kharazmi in Maqtal Al-Husain V1 P97.
[103] Bihar Al-Anwar V26 P349 H22. Ghayatol Maram P19 H21. Arbaeen lel Montajab Al-Deen H9.

O Anas, what made you disobey me and ignore everything that I said about Ali bin Abi Taleb🖑 until you received the punishment? If Ali🖑 does not forgive you, you will not even smell Paradise. (And if you want his forgiveness) Announce and tell people that Ali🖑, his progeny, and their lovers are the "SAABEQUN", they are the first ones in Paradise. The lovers (of Ali🖑) are the neighbours of God's friends in Paradise. God's friends are Hamza (the Prophet's uncle), Jaafar (the Prophet's cousin), and Hasan and Husain🖑. As for Ali🖑, he is the SEDDIQ AL-AKBAR (the most truthful), the truthful one. Those who love him need not fear the Day of Judgement.[104]

Virtue #90

Abul Hasan Ali bin Mohammad bin Alawea Al-Mostamli narrated from Abu Abdullah Mohammad bin Ahmad, from Hamdan bin Yahya, from Mohammad bin Sadagha, from Musa bin Jaafar (7th Imam), from Jaafar bin Mohammad (6th Imam), from his father (5th Imam), from Ali bin Husain (4th Imam), from his father (Imam Husain)🖑, who said:

The Messenger of God🖑 said:

When God created Paradise, He ordered Paradise to decorate itself and it did. Then God said to Paradise, "I swear to My Magnificence that I did not create you except for the believers. May there be bliss and happiness for you and your inhabitants!"

Then the Prophet🖑 said to Ali🖑, 'O Ali, Paradise was not created except for you and your Shia.'[105]

Virtue #91

Abu Mohammad Husain Al-Faresi Al-Bai' narrated from Ahmad bin Mohammad, from Mohammad bin Mansour, from Mohammad bin Ismail, from Wakeh, from Sufyan, from Ash'aab, from Akrama, from Ibn Abbas, who said:

Ibn Abbas said, "I would have given the world to have had the Messenger of God🖑 make the statement he made about Ali bin Abi Taleb🖑 about me."

---

[104] Kharazmi in Manaqeb P32. and his Maqtal V1 P40. Kashf Al-Ghommah V1 P104. Ghayatol maram P580 H27. Madinat Al-Maajez P51 H103. Misbah Al-Anwar P137 . Bihar Al-Anwar V68 P40 H84.
[105] Ghayatol Maram P587 H90.

So people asked Ibn Abbas, "What was the statement?"

Ibn Abbas replied, "The Prophet﴾ﷺ﴿ told Ali bin Abi Taleb﴾عليه السلام﴿, 'You are from me and I am from you; your progeny is from us and we are from them; your Shia are from us and we are from them, and your Shia will enter Paradise five hundred years before the others.'"[106]

Virtue #92

Ibrahim bin Al-Modhari Al-Khayyat narrated from Ahmad bin Mohammad bin Saeed Al-Rafaa Al-Baghdadi, from Ahmad bin Aleel, from Abdullah bin Dawud Al-Ansari, from Musa bin Ali Al-Qorashi, from Qanbar bin Ahmad bin Qanbar, from his father, from his grandfather, Qanbar, the servant of Ali bin Abi Taleb, from Kaab bin Noufel, from Bilal bin Hamama, who said:

The Prophet﴾ﷺ﴿ came to the people one day and his face was beaming like the moon.

So Abd-Al-Rahman Al-A'wf asked the Prophet﴾ﷺ﴿, "Why is your face beaming like this?"

The Prophet﴾ﷺ﴿ replied:

> I received good news from God about my brother and my cousin and my daughter. God married Ali to Fatema and he ordered Rezwan (the Keeper of Paradise) to shake the tree of TOUBA. Rezwan shook the tree, and for every lover of my family, one leaf fell from the tree. Then Rezwan gave each one of the leaves to an angel that was made of light.
>
> On the Day of Judgement, these angels will call and say 'O lovers of Ali bin Abi Taleb, come and collect your belongings.' So all those who love my family and I will receive a leaf.
>
> These leaves are the passes that save people from Hell; they are given to people as a reward for loving Ali bin Abi Taleb and Fatema, my daughter, and their sons.[107]

---

[106] Ghayatol Maram P459 H35.
[107] Bihar Al-Anwar V27 P117 H96. Ghayatol maram P586 H85. Tarikh Baghdad V4 P210 H1897. Osad Al-Ghabah V1 P206. Al-Sawaegh Al-Mohreghe P103. Al-Fathael Al-Khamsa V2 P147.

Virtue #93

Zakariyya narrated from Abdullah bin Muslim, from Al-Mofadhal bin Saleh, from Jabir bin Yazid, from Zathan, from Salman and Ibn Abbas, who said:

The Messenger of Godﷺ said:

On the night of Meraj I approached my Lord and I "was at a distance of two bows or nearer still" (53:9). He spoke to me between the two AQEEQ (carnelian) mountains and said,

> O Ahmad, I created you and Ali from My own light, and I created these two mountains from the light of Ali's face. I swear by My Magnificence that I have created these two mountains to be a sign that is used to identify the believers. And I swore on Myself that I make it Haram to send to Hell those who wear the AQEEQ ring on their hands and follow Ali bin Abi Taleb.[108]

Virtue #94

Mohammad bin Hasan narrated from Isa bin Mihran, from Ubaidullah bin Musa, from Khalid bin Tahman Al-Khaffaf, from Saad bin Ganada Al-Owfi, from Zaid bin Arqam, from Aba Said Al-Khodri, who said:

The Messenger of Godﷺ said, "Ali bin Abi Taleb is the Master of Arabs."[109]

So the people asked the Prophetﷺ, "Are you not the Master of Arabs?"

The Prophetﷺ replied:

> I am the Master of human beings and Ali is the Master of Arabs. God loves those who love Ali and follow him, and (God) guides them to the right path. God makes those who hate Ali and those who fight him deaf and blind.

> Ali's HAQQ (right) is my HAQQ, and following him is following me, except that there is no prophet after me. Those who abandon him abandon me, and those who abandon me abandon God.

---

[108] Ghayatol Maram P7 H13.

[109] Note from Translator: Referring to Imam Ali ؏ as the Master of the Arabs in this HADITH means he is the master of the best of the believers.

I am the city of knowledge and Ali is the door of the city. How is it possible for anyone to be guided to Paradise except through this door?

Ali is the best human being. Those who deny this are KAFERS.[110]

Virtue #95

The judge, Abu Mohammad Al-Hasan bin Mohammad bin Musa, narrated from Ali bin Thabet, from Hafs bin Omar, from Yahya bin Jaafar, from Abdul Rahman bin Ibrahim, from Malik bin Anas, from Nafi', from Abdullah bin Omar bin Al-Khattab, who said:

The Messenger of God ﷺ said:

God accepts the Salaat, the SIYAM (Fasting), and the efforts of those who love Ali bin Abi Taleb, and He answers their prayers.

Beware! God gives those who love Ali one city (in Paradise) for each vein in their body.

Beware! Those who love the family of the Prophet are safe from the judgement process, the scale, and from the bridge.

Beware! I guarantee Paradise in the neighbourhood of the prophets to those who love the family of the Prophet.

Beware! Those who die hating the family of the Prophet will have the following written between their eyes on the Day of Judgement, "Excluded from the Mercy of God."[111]

Virtue #96

Abu Abdullah Ahmad bin Mohammad bin Ayyoub narrated from Ali bin Mohammad bin Ayyenah bin Rowaida, from Bakr bin Ahmad and Ahmad bin Mohammad Al-Jarrah, from Ahmad bin Fadl Al-Ahwazi, from Bakr bin Ahmad, from Mohammad bin Ali (9th Imam), from his father (8th Imam), from Musa bin Jaafar (7th Imam), from his father (6th Imam), from Mohammad bin Ali

[110] Ghayatol Maram P543 H30. Amali Al-Sadough P317 H11. Amali of Tousi V2 P45 h21. Bihar Al-Anwar V40 P200 H2.
[111] Ghayatol Maram P580 H28 Bihar Al-Anwar V27 p120 H100. Manaqeb of Kharazmi P32. Maqtal Al-Husain of kharazmi V1 P40. Kashf Al-Ghomma V1 P104. Ershad Al-Gholoub P235. Lesan Al-Mizan V5 P62. Faraed Al-Semthain V2 P257 H526. Ehqaq Al-haq V7 P161. Arjahol Mataleb P526. Aalam Al-deen P284.

(5th Imam), from Fatema, Imam Husain's daughter, from her father, Imam Husain and from her uncle, Imam Hasan, from the Commander of the Believers, Ali bin Abi Taleb, who said:

The Messenger of God said:

> When I entered Paradise, I saw some different coloured horses under a tree that was decorated with jewels. I saw HUR AL-EEN in the middle of the tree, and I saw Rezwan (the Keeper of Paradise) on top of the tree. So I asked Jibraeel to whom the tree belonged.

He (Jibraeel) replied:

> It belongs to your cousin, Ali bin Abi Taleb. When God orders His creatures to enter Paradise, the Shia of Ali will be brought to this tree. They will decorate themselves from the jewels of the tree and they will ride the different coloured horses. Then the caller will call, 'These are the Shia of Ali. They were patient when they were hurt in the world, so they are being rewarded with generosity today.'[112]

Virtue #97

Ahmad bin Mohammad bin Husain narrated from Wazirah bin Mohammad bin Wazirah, from his grandfather, Wazirah bin Mohammad Al-Ghasani, from Ali bin Musa Al-Redha (8th Imam), from his father (7th Imam), from Jaafar bin Mohammad (6th Imam), from his father (5th Imam), from Ali bin Al-Husain (4th Imam), from his father (Imam Husain), who said:

The Messenger of God said:

As I was going up on the night of Meraj, I met my father, Nuh. He asked me, "O Mohammad, whom did you appoint as caliph on your nation?"

I replied, "Ali bin Abi Taleb."

Nuh said, "What an excellent caliph you appointed."

Then I met my brother, Musa, who asked me, "O Mohammad, whom did you appoint as caliph on your nation?"

I replied, "Ali bin Abi Taleb."

---

[112] Ghayatol maram P19 H22. Bihar Al-Anwar V27 P120 H101. Al-Yagheen P63. Managen kharazmi P32. Maqtal AL-Husain Kharazmi V1 P40. Misbah Al-Anwar p61. Aalam Al-Deen P285

Musa said, "What an excellent caliph you appointed."

Then I met my brother, Isa, who asked me, "O Mohammad, whom did you appoint as caliph on your nation?"

I replied, "Ali bin Abi Taleb."

Isa said, "What an excellent caliph you appointed."

Then I asked Jibraeel, "Why have I not seen my father, Ibrahim?"

So Jibraeel took me to an area where I saw Ibrahim by a tree that had nipples like the nipples of sheep. There were lots of babies sucking on the nipples of this tree, thereby receiving their sustenance. Every time a nipple would fall out of a baby's mouth, Ibrahim would put it back in their mouth.

Ibrahim asked me, "O Mohammad, whom did you appoint as caliph on your nation?"

I replied, "Ali bin Abi Taleb."

Ibrahim said, "What an excellent caliph you appointed. O Mohammad, I asked God to make me responsible for giving sustenance to the babies of Ali's 🕮 Shia. So I am responsible for their sustenance until the Day of Judgement." [113]

Virtue #98

The judge, Abul Hasan Mohammad bin Uthman bin Abdullah Al-Nasibi, narrated from Jaafar bin Mohammad Al-Aalawy, from Abdullah bin Ahmad, from Mohammad bin Ziad, from Mofadhal bin Amr, from Jaafar bin Mohammad (6th Imam), from his father (5th Imam), from Ali bin Husain (4th Imam), from his father (3rd Imam), from the Commander of the Believers 🕮, who said:

I was sitting in an open area and people were sitting around me.

Then someone stood up and said, "O Commander of the Believers 🕮, it is God that has made your status so low, and your father will be tortured in Hell."

I replied:

---

[113] Ghayatol maram P69 H21. Bihar AlAnwar V27 P121 H102.

Be quiet! May God shut your mouth[114]. I swear to God, who sent
Mohammad as a prophet, that if my father intercedes for all of
the sinners on earth, God will accept it. How can my father be in
Hell, while I, his son, am the one who divides between Paradise
and Hell? I swear to God, who sent Mohammad as a prophet,
my father's light on the Day of Judgement exceeds the light of all
creatures except the light of five lights: the light of
Mohammad, my (Imam Ali's) light, the light of Fatema,
the light of Hasan and Husain, and the light of the Imams from
the sons of Husain. Beware that Abu Taleb's light is from
our lights. God created his light two thousand years before He
created Adam.[115]

Virtue #99

Al-Moaafi bin Zakariyya Abul Faraj narrated from Mohammad bin Ahmad bin
Abi Thalj, from Hasan bin Mohammad bin Bahram, from Yousef bin Musa Al-
Qattan, from Jurair, from Laith, from Mujahid, from Ibn Abbas, who said:

The Messenger of God said, "If all the trees were pens, and all the seas
were ink, and all the Jinn were counters, and all human beings were writers,
they would not be able to count the incredible virtues of Ali bin Abi Taleb."
[116]

Virtue #100

Abu Mohammad Al-Hasan bin Ahmad bin Mohammad Al-Majledi narrated
from Husain bin Mohammad bin Ishaq, from Mohammad bin Zakariyya, from
Jaafar bin Mohammad (6th Imam), from his father (5th Imam), from Ali bin
Husain (4th Imam), from his father (3rd Imam), from the Commander of the
Believers, who said:

The Messenger of God said:

---

[114] Note from Translator: Do not forget: Ali is with HAQQ and HAQQ is with Ali.
[115] Al-Hojja aala al-zahed P72. Al-Darajatol Rafeeah P50 .Amali Al-Tousi V1 P331 H58. Bisharat Al-
Mustafa p249. Al-Ehtejaj of Tabrasi V1 P340. Bihar Al-Anwar V35 P69 H3. Al-Ghadeer V7 P387 H3.
[116] Kanz Al-Ommal P128. Manaqeb Kharazmi P2. Kefayato Taleb P251. Faraed Al-Semthain V1 P16.
Lesan AL-Mizan V5 P62. Mizan AL-Eetedal V3 P467. Bihar Al-Anwar V4 P70 H105. Kashf Al-
Ghomma V1 H111. AL-Taraef P138 H216. Helyatol Abrar V1 P289. Yanabee Al-Mawaddah P121.
Ghayatol Maram P493 H1. Manaqeb Kharazmi P235. Arjah Al-Mataleb P11.Kashf Al-Haq V1 P108.
Arbaeen Al-Khozaee H38. Misbah Al-Anwar p121. Taweel Al-Ayat P888 H13. Mawaddat Al-Qurba
P55.

God has given so many incredible virtues to my brother, Ali bin Abi Taleb, that they are impossible to count. If someone mentions one of his virtues while believing in it, God will forgive all of his past and future sins. If someone writes one of his virtues, angels will seek forgiveness for him for as long as that written text continues to exist. If someone listens to one of his virtues, God will forgive all of the sins that he has committed using his ears. If someone reads a book about his virtues, God will forgive all of the sins that he has committed using his eyes.

Looking at Ali bin Abi Taleb is worshipping God, and mentioning him is worshipping God.

God does not accept the beliefs of anyone who does not accept Ali's WILAYAT, and who does not renounce his enemies.[117]

---

[117] Bihar Al-Anwar V26 P229 H10. Manaqeb Kharazmi P2. Kefayat Al-Taleb P252. Faraed Al-Semthain V1 P19. Mizan Al-Eetedal V3 p467. Amali Al-Sadough P119 H9. Jamee Al-Akhbar P17. Taweel Al-Ayat P888. Kashf Al-Haq V1 P108. Yanbee Al-mawadda P121. Ghayatol Maram P293 H2. Al-Mohtazar P98. Kashf Al-Ghommah V1 P112.

About the Book

In the name of Allah, Most Gracious, Most Merciful.

The incredible virtues of Ali bin Abi Taleb are enumerable. It is as the Holy Prophet says, "If all the trees were pens, and all the seas were ink, and all the Jinn were counters, and all human beings were writers, they would not be able to count the incredible virtues of Ali bin Abi Taleb."

His incredible virtues are filled in Sunni books. Some of the most prominent Sunni scholars like Ahmad bin Hanbal, Esmaeel bin Ishaq, Al-Nesaee and Abu Ali Al-Neishabouri have stated that, "No one has narrated any HADITH with such reliable and authentic sources for any of the companions of the Prophet like the AHADITH narrated about Ali bin Abi Taleb."

The following Sunni books are some of the references used in this book:

1. Al-Esteeab
2. Sawaee Al-Mohraqa
3. Nour Al-Absar
4. Fath Al-Bari
5. Mostadrak Ala Al-Sahihain
6. Tafsir Al-Thaalabi
7. Manqeb Al-Kharazmi
8. Tabaqat Hanabela
9. Al-Kamel Ibn Atheer
10. Kefayat Al-Taleb
11. Riyadh Al-Nazerat
12. Nozam Dorar Al-Semthain
13. Tahzib al-Tahzib
14. Tarikh Al-Kholafaa
15. Sirat Al-Halabiya
16. Esaaf Al-Raghebeen
17. Al-Rowaz Al-Azhar
18. Miftah Al-Naja
19. Yanabee Al-Mawaddah
20. Tajheez Al-Jeysh
21. Maqsad Al-Taleb
22. Fath Al-Ola
23. Sharh Jame Al-Saghir Al-Manawi
24. Shawahed Al-Tanzeel
25. Tarikh Dameshq
26. Manaqeb Ahmad bin Hanbal
27. Manaqeb Al-Ashera lel Ghashbandi
28. Merqat Al-Mafateeh fi Sharh Mishkat Al-Masabeeh

29. Al-Mokhtar fi Al-Manaqeb Al-Akhyar
30. Ethaf Zowe Al-Nejaba
31. Zolomat Abi Riyah
32. Tabaqat Al-Malekiyya
33. Madakhel al-Qirawanee
34. Sharh Resalat Al-Halabi
35. Wasilat Al-Najat
36. Tafrih AL-Ahbab
37. Manal Al-Taleb fi Manaqen Ali bin Abi Taleb
38. Barqiyyah Al-Mohammadiya
39. Ehqaq Al-Haqq

Both Sunni and Shia scholars have used Ibn Shazan as a reference and relied on his books and research.

The following are some of the Sunni scholars that have relied on this specific book and have quoted their AHADITH from it:

1. Al-Hafez Abu Moayyed Al-Mowaffaq bin Ahmad bin Mohammad bin Al-Bakri Al-Hanafi known as Akhtab Al-Khawarazm
2. Al-Hafez Al-Shahid Abu Obaidullah Mohammad bin Yousef bin Mohammad Al-Qorashi Al-Kanji Al-Shafiee who was killed in the mosque of Damascus because he wrote a book called Kefayat Al-Taleb that had some positive views about Shia.
3. Al-Mohaddeth Ibrahim bin Mohammad bin Moayyed bin Abdullah bin Ali Al-Hamawaynee

Many of our Shia scholars including, Abul Fath Mohammad bin Ali bin Uthman Al-Karajee, Seyed Radhi Ibn Tawous, Al-Majlesi, Seyed Hashem Al-Bahrani, and Allama Sheykh Abdul Husain Al-Amini, have based their books and views on this book and other publications of Ibn Shazan.

Narrators used in this book match the ones that the following great Shia scholars have trusted and used:

1. The scholar, Abi Jaafar Mohammad bin Ali bin Husain bin Babewey Al-Qummi
2. The scholar, Abi Mohammad, Jaafar bin Ahmad bin Ali Al-Qummi
3. The scholar, Abi Al-Qasem Ali bin Mohammad bin Ali Al-Khazzaz Al-Qummi
4. The scholar, Abi Abdullah Mohammad bin Mohammad bin Noman Al-Mofid
5. The scholar, Abi Al-Abbas Ahmad bin Ali Al-Najashi

The following is a list of the narrators on whom the above Shia scholars have relied in their own works (that can be found in this book):

1. Abu Mohammad Ibrahim bin Mohammad Al-Mathari Al-Khayyat
2. Abul Hasan Ahmad bin Al-Hasan, Al-Dhak, Al-Razi
3. The Nishapuri Ahmad bin Al-Hasan bin Mohammad
4. Ahmad bin Ali bin Al-Hasan bin Shazan Al-Fami Al-Qummi (His father)
5. Abul Hasan Ahmad bin Mohammad bin Ahmad bin Tarkhan Al-Kendi Algrani
6. Ahmad bin Mohammad bin Al-Husain
7. Ahmad bin Mohammad bin Saeed bin Oqda
8. Ahmad bin Mohammad bin Suleiman bin Al-Hasan bin Bakeer bin Aayan bin Sonan Abu Ghalib Al-Zarari
9. Abu Abdullah Ahmad bin Mohammad bin Ubaidullah bin Al-Hasan Aiaash bin Ibrahim bin Ayyoub bin Al-Johri
10. Ahmad bin Mohammad bin Imran Al-Jarrah
11. Ahmad bin Mohammad bin Musa bin Urwah
12. Abu Mohammad Jaafar bin Ahmad bin Al-Husain Al-Shashi
13. Abul Qassem Jaafar bin Mohammad bin Qoloeh (His Uncle)
14. Abul Qassem Jaafar bin Mohammad bin Masrur
15. Al-Hasan bin Ahmad bin Sokhtoeh
16. Abu Mohammad Al-Hasan bin Ahmad bin Mohammad Al-Mogldi
17. Al-Sharif Al-Hasan bin Hamza bin Ali bin Abdullah bin Mohammad bin Al-Hasan Al-Husain bin Ali bin Al-Husain bin Ali bin Abi Taleb Abu Mohammad Al-Taabari.
18. Al-Sharif Al-Naqeeb, Abu Mohammad Al-Hasan bin Mohammad Al-Alwy Al-Hussayni
19. The judge, Abu Mohammad Al-Hasan bin Mohammad bin Musa
20. Abu Abdullah Al-Husain bin Ahmad bin Mohammad bin Ahwal
21. The virtuous sheikh, Abu Abdullah Al-Husain bin Abdullah Al-Qutiei
22. The Persian, Abu Mohammad Al-Husain Al-Baye
23. Abu Abdullah Al-Husain bin Mohammad bin Isaac bin Khetab Al-Soti
24. Al-Husain bin Mohammad bin Mihran Al-Damghani
25. The Chief of Justice Abu Abdullah Al-Husain bin Harun Al-Daabi
26. Sahl bin Ahmad bin Abdullah bin Ahmad bin Sahl Al-Dibagi Al-Taraeqi Al-Koufi
27. Zakariyya Talha bin Ahmad bin Talha bin Mohammad Al-Sarram Al-Nishaburi
28. Abu Ahmad Abdulaziz bin Jaafar bin Mohammad bin Qoloeh
29. Sheikh Al-Saleh Abu Mohammad Abdullah bin Al-Husain
30. Abul Qassem Abdullah bin Mohammad bin Isaac bin Suleiman bin Hanana Al-Bazaz
31. Abu Mohammad Abdullah bin Yousef bin Mamoeh Al-Asbahani
32. Abul Qassem Ubaidullah bin Al-Hasan bin Mohammad Al-Sakwy
33. Abul Hasan Ali bin Ahmad bin Motoeh Al-Makri Al-Wahedi

34. Ali bin Al-Husain bin Ali bin Al-Hasan Abul Hasan Al-Nahwy Al-Razi
35. Bin Mohammad Motola, Al-Qalansi
36. Abul Hasan Ali bin Mohammad Al-Mokteb Al-Loghawy Al-Razi
37. Abu Hafs Amr bin Ibrahim bin Ahmad bin Katheer Al-Makri known as Al-knaey
38. Al-Hafez Abu Bakr Mohammad bin Ahmad bin Al-Husain bin Al-Qassem bin Al-Ghatrif Al-Jorjani
39. Al-Sharif Abu Jaafar Mohammad bin Ahmad bin Mohammad bin Isa Al-Alawy
40. Abul Hasan Mohammad bin Jaafar bin Mohammad bin Al-Najjar Al-Kufi Al-Nahwy Al-Tameemi
41. The great sheikh Mohammad bin Al-Hasan bin Ahmad bin Al-Walid
42. Abul Tayyeb Mohammad bin Al-Husain Al-Timli
43. Mohammad bin Hammad bin Bashir
44. Mohammad bin Hamid bin Al-Husain bin Hamid bin Al-Risbia Al-Lokhmi Al-Jarrar
45. Mohammad bin Said, Abul Faraj
46. Mohammad bin Said Al-Dahqan
47. The Scholar Abu Bakr Mohammad bin Abdullah bin Hamdun Al Fadl
48. Mohammad bin Abdullah bin Mohammad bin Ubaidullah bin Al-Bohlul bin Matar bin Mutleb bin Matar bin Abul Fadhl Al-Sheibanee
49. Mohammad bin Abdullah bin Abdullah the Al-Hafez
50. Mohammad bin Abdullah bin Ubaiduallah bin Murra
51. The Judge, Abul Husain Mohammad bin Uthman bin Abdullah Al-Nasibi
52. Mohammad bin Ali bin Husain bin bin Musa bin Babewey "Al-Sadough"
53. Abu Abdullah Mohammad bin Ali bin Zanjawiyah
54. Mohammad bin Ali bin Sukkar
55. Abul Husain Mohammad bin Ali bin Al-Mofadhal bin Homam Al-Koufi
56. Mohammad bin Fadhl bin Tamam Al-Zayyat
57. Mohammad bin Emad Al-Tostary
58. Mohammad bin Mohammad bin Morrat
59. Abul Faraj Mohammad bin Muzaffar bin Ahmad bin Saeed Al-Daghagh
60. Abul Faraj Mohammad bin Muzaffar bin Qays Al-Moqari
61. Abu Abdullah Mohammad bin Wahban Al-Hannad
62. Abu Sahl Mahmoud bin Amr bin Mahmoud Al-Askary
63. The judge, Abul Faraj Al-Moaafi bin Zakariyya bin Yahya Al-Nahrawani
64. Al-Shaykh Nouh bin Ahmad bin Ayman
65. Abu Mohammad Haroon bin Musa bin Ahmad bin Saeed Al-Talakbari
66. Abu Mohammad bin Fareed Al-Bushanji